THE STORY VINE

THE STORY VINE

A Source Book of Unusual and Easy-to-Tell
Stories from Around the World

Anne Pellowski

Illustrated by Lynn Sweat

Macmillan Publishing Company
New York

Collier Macmillan Publishers
London

Macmillan books are available at special discounts for bulk purchases for sales promotions, premiums, fund-raising, or educational use. Special editions or book excerpts can also be created to specification. For details, contact:

Special Sales Director
Macmillan Publishing Company
866 Third Avenue
New York, N.Y. 10022

Macmillan Publishing Company
866 Third Avenue, New York, N.Y. 10022
Collier Macmillan Canada, Inc.

Printed in the United States of America

Book design by Constance Ftera

10   9   8   7   6

Library of Congress Cataloging in Publication Data

Pellowski, Anne.
  The story vine.

  Bibliography: p.
  1. Story-telling.   2. Tales.   3. Children's stories.
I. Sweat, Lynn.   II. Title.
LB1042.P43   1984   372.6′4   83-26756
ISBN 0-02-770590-0

Dedicated to
Jeff, Eric, Kevin, Janie,
Kyla, Keith, Steven, Abby,
and all the others to come.

Contents

Acknowledgments

Emily Power, Molly Power and Anna Rodel for permission to use their version of ''Cat's Cradle,'' pages 43–44.

Asian Cultural Centre for UNESCO (Tokyo) for permission to reproduce the picture-drawing song, ''Bō ga Ippon,'' page 57, taken from *Folk and Traditional Music of Asia for Children,* produced under the Asian Co-production Programme.

Cornell University Press (Ithaca, N.Y.) for figures in the chart on pages 62–63, adapted from Nancy D. Munn's *Walbiri Iconography,* © 1973. Used by permission of the publisher.

Edwards and Shaw (Sydney) for permission to adapt the story ''The Rainbow Snake'' from Roland Robinson's *Legend and Dreaming,* © 1952.

Routledge & Kegan Paul (London) for permission to adapt the title story from Hugh Tracey's book *The Lion on the Path and Other Stories,* © 1967.

Editions de l'Amitié (G. T. Rageot) for permission to translate and adapt the story ''Rabbit and Hyena Play the Sanza,'' from René Guillot's *Au Pays des Bêtes Sauvages,* © 1948.

Among the Lega of Zaire and the Sambui of
Angola, and other groups as well, it was
common for itinerant storytellers to use
a vine or string to which they had attached
an object matching each tale they told.
The listeners pointed to one of the objects
and, upon payment, could then hear the story.

Introduction

When I first began telling stories more than twenty-five years ago, I told only stories from books, using a straightforward narrative style. This is still one of my favorite ways of telling a story.

However, after some ten years as a storyteller, I began to research the history and background of all kinds of storytelling, in many different areas of the world. Whenever I could, I observed live storytellers as they performed for an audience. I soon realized that there were, and are, many different styles and methods of telling a story.

On my first trip to Africa, for example, I experienced a number of vibrant storytelling sessions in which the thumb piano was used. I bought a few thumb pianos, adapted two stories as best I could from my memory of the performances, and then began telling the two stories to groups in the United States. The response was so positive, I have been using the two stories ever since.

Subsequently I discovered other ways of telling stories, in many cases using unusual objects, and gradually I began to include more of this type of storytelling in my repertoire. Because many of these stories are short and have an unusual twist, I find them ideal for alternating with the longer, more traditional narratives I still use in a storytelling session.

I also discovered that these stories are a remarkably successful method of introducing other cultures in a positive way. To introduce various aspects of Chinese culture to a group of first-graders, I once told the story of "Why the Years Are Named for Animals." Five years later, one of the children who had heard the story commented: "I like the Chinese because I like how they got the different names of animals for the years."

But above all, I enjoy telling these stories because they are interesting and entertaining to me, as a teller. And the many audiences with whom I have shared them have seemed to agree.

The stories in this book represent the objects that I carry around on my personal "story vine." The vine is imaginary, but I often string the objects out in a line on a table or shelf. Frequently a member of the audience will point to an object and ask for that story, in much the same way that the Lega listeners requested a tale from the storytelling vine.

Other storytellers have asked me for the sources of these unusual stories, so that they might try them out. This book has been written as an answer to those requests.

It is not easy to find stories of the types included in this book, and it is harder still to locate their origins. In order to tell them effectively, one often has to piece together several fragments, and even to embroider and invent. This is particularly true of the string stories, in which only key words and phrases are left in the memory of the people from whom the string figures were taken down. However, it is my belief that if one selects carefully from the motifs extant among the people, one can construct a tale that at least does not do violence to the beliefs and attitudes of that society, even though it might be somewhat removed from any story actually told by its members.

Some storytellers may wonder why there are no stories in this collection that do *not* use accompanying objects, music, or visual devices. My answer is that there are many very fine collections of such stories. I myself have drawn a good portion of my repertoire from a number of them. I would rather see the storyteller search out those collections, or listen to tellers bringing the tales in them to life, than be limited to the few that could be included here.

Story selection is one of the most difficult parts of storytelling. No two tellers can or should have the same repertoire. At the end of this book I have listed some of the stories and collections that are my personal favorites.

In their book *Yes and No Stories,* George and Helen Papashvily wrote: "A story is a letter that comes to us from yesterday." My hope is that storytellers using this book and consulting my lists will explore all the stories and select only those few to tell that seem to be like letters personally addressed to them.

PART ONE

String Stories

Strings can be described as one of the earlier forms of the book. Quite a number of peoples are known to have used strings for record-keeping and historical accounts. The most famous of these string "books" were the *quipu* of the Incas: long strips of leather knotted and twisted in patterns that told of events in the life of the tribe.

Today, string figures are still created in many parts of the world. In some places there are surviving fragments of the stories, myths, chants, or songs that accompanied them.

The peoples of the Pacific region and of Africa have particularly rich traditions of string figures. In some cases the figures are given symbolic names, more often than not related to the configuration of the stars and planets, or something in nature. Other figures have names that aptly fit the shapes created by the movement of the strings.

In order to tell string stories, one has to study carefully the typical patterns and their names in each culture and then try to re-create the tales imaginatively from the bits and pieces recorded by ethnographers, folklorists, and string figure hobbyists. Also, one must practice them enough so that the telling is accompanied by smoothly executed patterns that look utterly simple to do, but often are not!

However, the person who attempts telling string stories will soon find that they are an almost magical, universal entrée into social encounters with virtually any group, even where there is a language barrier.

Once the storyteller has successfully mastered a few string stories, such as those given here, he or she should have no difficulty in creating others by using the source books mentioned at the end of this section, or by visiting areas of the world where string storytelling is still a common form of entertainment.

How to Make Good Strings for Use in Telling String Stories

For best results, it is important to have the correct length of string for each story. Soft, white butcher's string is fine, but take care that it is not the kind that twists and curls easily.

Strings of different colors enable partially sighted audience members to distinguish the figures more easily. They also enhance the stories. For instance, the string for the Snake and Lizard stories could be of multicolored green. A black string for ''The Mosquito'' adds immeasurably to the illusion.

Any type of yarn that is smooth will also work well, provided you braid it. Cut three equal strands of yarn into the length suggested for each story. Clip the three strands together four inches from one end. Have someone hold the end taut while you braid the strands until you come to the last four inches at the other end.Ⓐ

Tie two of the strands together, over the third, at each end, so that they will not unravel.Ⓑ

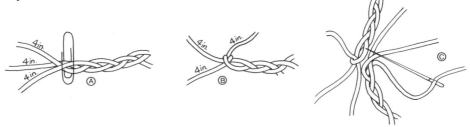

Using a darning needle, weave each strand, one by one, into the *op-*

4

posite end of the string, beginning at the point beyond the knot where the braid starts. Do the same with the three strands on the other end. Cut off any loose yarn ends remaining after you have finished. You need not tie the ends before cutting; just make sure that you have woven in at least three of the four inches for each strand.©

Still another method of constructing a circular string is that used by the Australian storyteller Kel Watkins, and also recommended by Joost Elffers and Michael Schuyt in their book.

In that method, nylon cord is melded together by melting the two ends and then quickly fusing them together. For his very complex figures, Mr. Watkins uses two pieces of nylon cord, each of a different color. His figures often end up with one color as the border and the other color comprising the figure within. Such two-color strings are very effective, and are worth the effort, for those storytellers who have progressed beyond the simple figures.

The Mosquito

This string figure has been called "The Fly" by (among others) the Patomana Indians of Guyana, the Melanesians of New Caledonia, and some of the people in Ghana. In Uganda it was known as "The Locust."

I have followed the directions given by Lyle Alexander Dickey in his book *String Figures from Hawaii* but have added the part about weaving. That illusion can easily be created by exaggerating and repeating the in and out movements and by keeping the hands in constant motion, even though the string remains in the same places.

The story is most effective with young children between the ages of three and eight. They will duck and try to avoid the "mosquito" and then, at the end, ask in wonder: "Where did it go?"

Recommended string length before knotting: 40 inches (100 cm)
Recommended strand length when braiding yarn: 50 inches (125 cm)

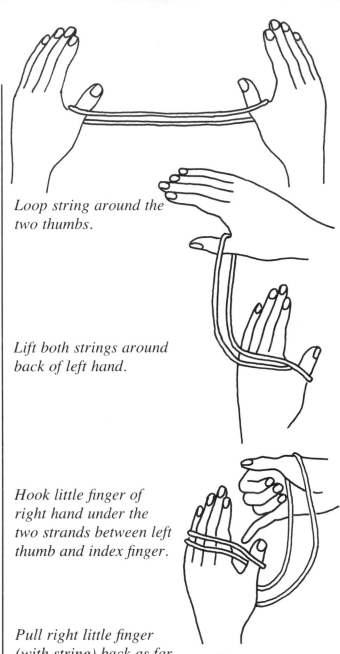

A woman sat weaving one day, when suddenly she heard a buzzing noise nearby.

Loop string around the two thumbs.

She looked up and saw nothing, so she continued her weaving,

Lift both strings around back of left hand.

in

Hook little finger of right hand under the two strands between left thumb and index finger.

and out,

Pull right little finger (with string) back as far as it will go. Keep strings taut, moving them as far down on the fingers and thumbs as they will go.

in and out.

The buzzing noise now got louder and the woman looked around again, but seeing nothing, continued her weaving.

Bring left little finger toward right palm and from the top, curl it under the two strands running from right thumb across the palm.

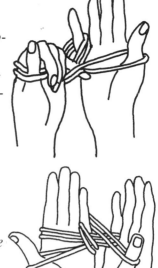

In and out,

Move the left little finger, with string, back into position, so the hands are side by side, palms facing you. There should be almost no space between the hands.

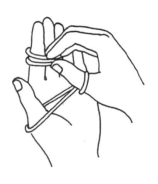

up and around.

With the right thumb and index finger, pick up the two strands of string running from the left palm to the back of the left hand.
Bring the two strings over all four fingers of the left hand and let go of them.

Suddenly the buzzing grew very loud. The woman looked at her weaving and saw—

a giant mosquito!

Quickly wiggle both hands back and forth, tightening the knot in the middle so that the figure ends up looking like a big mosquito. If necessary, use your right index finger to ease the knot to the center.

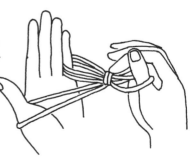

The mosquito began to buzz around her head. It buzzed into her ears and under her chin. It buzzed past her eyes and the tip of her nose. It buzzed in her hair and down her cheek. It was driving her crazy!

"I am going to catch that mosquito," said the woman. She waited until the mosquito flew right in front of her. Then she clapped her hands over it—

and the mosquito

was gone!

Move the "mosquito" close to the ears, chins, eyes, noses, hair, cheeks, etc., of the individual children in the front rows of the audience.

Move two hands with "mosquito" all around through the air and end up right in front of your face.

Clap hands together.

As hands begin to move apart, point little fingers slightly downward, releasing strings from little fingers as quickly and inconspicuously as possible. The "mosquito" will be gone.

The Farmer and His Yams

This string trick is known in many parts of the world. The story attached to it changes from place to place. A Japanese librarian told me she learned it as a child, under the name "Train." As each loop was put on the fingers, a car was added to the train, starting with the engine and ending with the caboose. When it was time for the train to move on, the engineer got up steam (the loop was taken off the left thumb) and slowly the train chugged off, making the "cars" disappear one by one into the tunnel.

In her book *String Figures and How to Make Them*, C. F. Jayne mentions several versions that are called "Cat and Mouse," or simply "Mouse," as played by different groups of people in the Philippines, in Africa, in Alaska, and other parts of the Americas.

I first tried telling it by using the version in W. W. R. Ball's book *String Figures* and gradually the story evolved after I had told it many times in various places. While I was sharing the story at a school in Tonga in 1978, the children helped to move the tale along by calling out what was happening. It was then I hit upon the final details, such as the farmer going to bed, falling asleep, getting out of bed, and so on. I have been telling the story in this way ever since.

The storyteller must practice the trick until it can be performed smoothly and must pay careful attention to the timing of voice and string movement. When it is done well, this story never fails to bring a gasp of delighted surprise from the audience.

Recommended string length before knotting: 54 inches (135 cm)
Recommended strand length when braiding yarn: 65 inches (165 cm)

There was once a farmer who had a field of yams. He went out one day and saw that his yams were ready for harvest.

Drape string over back of left hand. Make sure knot is at bottom if you use knotted string. Wave fingers lightly to indicate yam plants.

So he dug up some yams,

Bring right index finger from underneath left side of front hanging string (the one closest to you) and catch hold of that portion of the string between left thumb and index finger.

and then

With right index finger, pull loop down and toward you, until loop is about three inches long.

put them in a sack,

Twist the loop once clockwise *and then place loop over left index finger.*

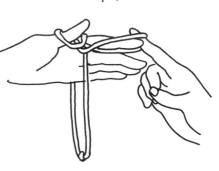

10

and tied it tight.

The farmer now had a fine sack of yams. But he saw that there were still yams left in the field so he went out,

dug up more yams,

put them in a sack,

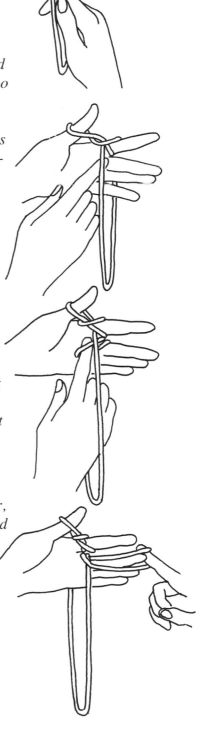

With right hand, grasp both strands of string hanging below left hand and pull until there is no slack in loop. Hold up left hand for all to see, making sure string stays in place. Place right index finger under the front palm string.

Push right index finger between left index and middle fingers and curl tip over the loose back string. With right index finger, pull string back through in a loop about three inches long.

Using right index finger, twist loop clockwise and then slip loop over left middle finger.

11

and tied it tight.

The farmer now had two bags of yams. But he saw there were still quite a few yams in his field, so even though it was a hot day, he continued to dig

until he had a big pile of yams.

He put them in a sack

With right hand, grasp both strands of hanging string and again pull until there is no slack in loop. Show left hand, keeping string in place.

Place right index finger under the front palm string.

Push right index finger between left middle and ring fingers and curl tip over loose back string. With right index finger, pull string back through in a loop about three inches long.

Using right index finger, twist loop clockwise and then slip loop over left ring finger.

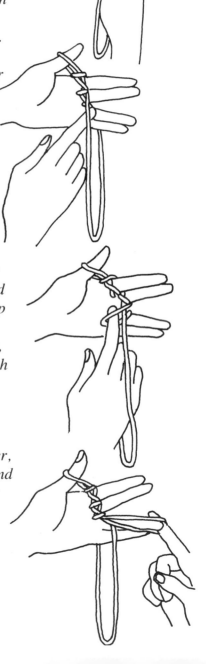

12

and tied it tight.

The farmer looked proudly at his three sacks of yams, lined up in a row. He was tired but he saw there were still a few more yams left in the field and he wanted to harvest them all, so out he went again,

dug up the last of the yams,

put them in a sack,

With right hand, grasp both strands of hanging string and pull until loop is taut.

Hold left hand out for all to see, making sure string stays in place.

Place right index finger under the front palm string.

Push right index finger between left ring and little fingers and curl tip over loose back string. With right index finger pull string back in a loop about three inches long.

Using right index finger, twist loop clockwise and then slip loop over left little finger.

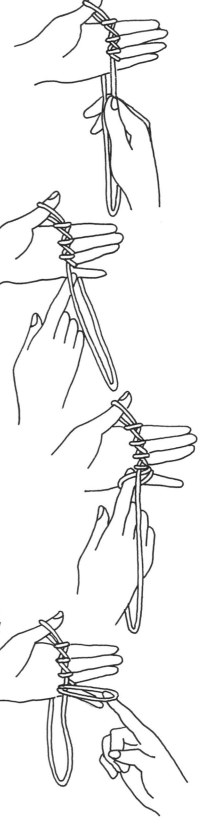

and tied it tight!

The farmer was very pleased with his four fine sacks of yams. But he was also worn out from having worked in the hot sun all day. It was already quite late, so the farmer decided to go to bed. He fell sound asleep.

In the middle of the night, he heard a noise and sat up in his bed!

"Maybe it's a thief," said the farmer. "I must go and see if someone is trying to steal my yams." So he got out of bed

With right hand, grasp both strands of hanging string and pull until loop is taut.
Hold left hand up for all to see, making sure thumb is up and string stays in place.

Slowly move left thumb downward until it is resting parallel with fingers.

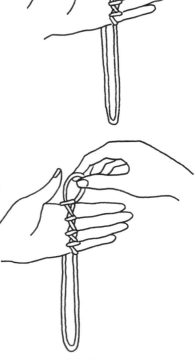

Lift left thumb up quickly.

Use right index finger and thumb to lift loop off left thumb. Let loop fall.

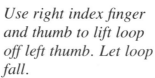

and went to look. First he looked in front of the sacks of yams. Nobody there.

Move left thumb up and down in front of "sacks" along line where palm meets fingers.

Then he went to look behind the sacks of yams, and while he was looking there,

Move left thumb toward back of hand, stretching it as far back as it will go.

that thief crept around to the front

With right hand, grasp front hanging string only, close to bottom edge of left hand.

and stole those sacks of yams!

Jerk downward on front hanging string and the "sacks" disappear. String ends up in right hand.

Grandmother's Candles

This intriguing series of tricks was known throughout Europe and the British Isles in the late nineteenth century. The figures often had different names from those given here and were sometimes put together in other sequences. For example, the "candles" segment was called "witch's broom" or simply "broom." The "scissors" was sometimes called "the pair of trousers."

I follow C. F. Jayne's version, but have expanded the words of the story to better suit the actions. This takes a bit of practice to do smoothly, matching the words precisely with the timing of the string figures, but it never fails to astound and please.

Recommended string length before knotting: 40 inches (100 cm)
Recommended strand length when braiding yarn: 50 inches (125 cm)

Before starting, have the string in this position. This is done by hanging the string over the left palm and then bringing one strand through between the index and middle fingers and the other through between the ring and little fingers. Make sure the string doesn't cross or twist at the back of the hand.

One day, Grandmother decided to make some candles. She brought out the string for the wicks, put the string

Using right thumb and index finger, pull palm string forward.

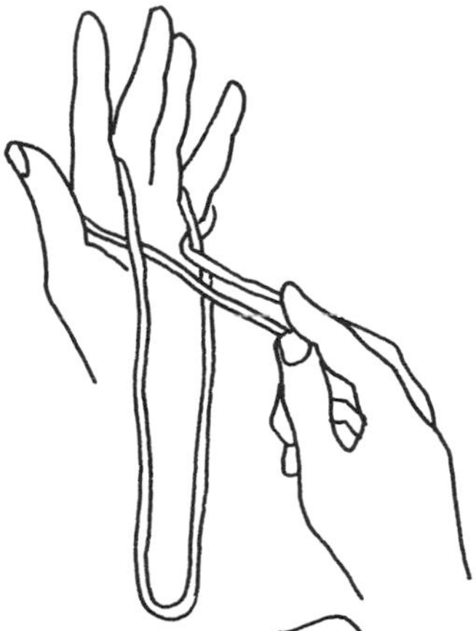

in the candle molds,

then up and over left middle and ring fingers,

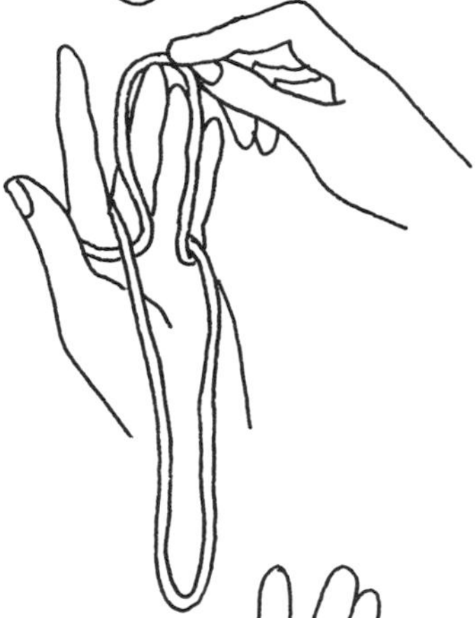

and all was ready.

and all the way back. Palm of left hand should look like this. Loops over left index and little fingers should be slightly loose.

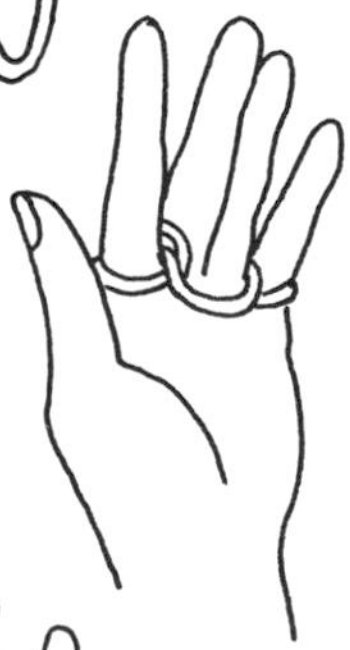

She poured the wax,

Insert right index finger in left index finger loop and right little finger in left little finger loop. Pull loops forward all the way.

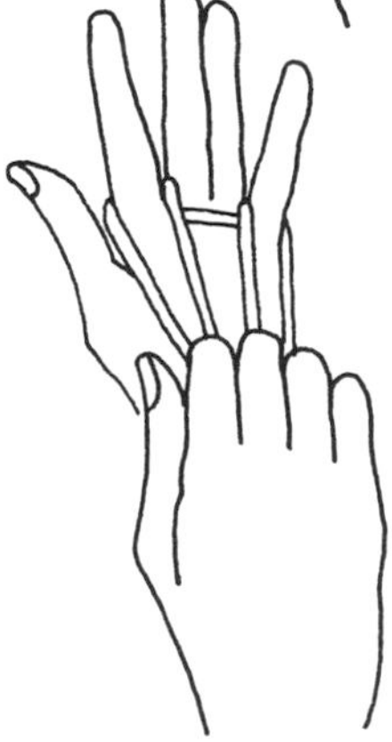

separated the candles in the molds,

Put left ring finger into drawn-out little finger loop and left middle finger into drawn-out index finger loop. Simultaneously, with right hand lift loops and pull backward, and curl all left fingers forward to form a fist.

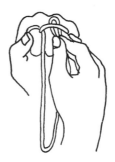

There should now be one strand between left index and middle fingers; two strands between middle and ring fingers; one strand between ring and little fingers.

and set them to dry.

Using right thumb and index finger, take bottom ends of both loops and insert them under string passing across back of left middle and ring fingers. Pull loops through all the way, until they are hanging down back of left hand.

18

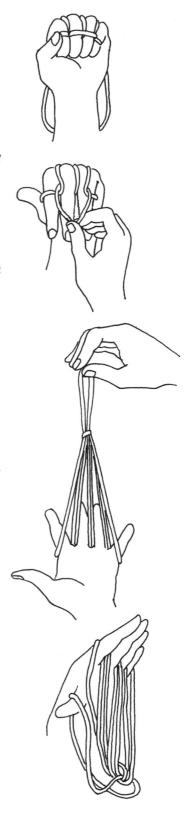

Left hand will look like this.

After a while, Grand-mother came to test the candles to see if they were hard. They were, so she took them out of the molds and hung them in a bunch to dry.

With right index finger and thumb, grasp string running across back of left middle and ring fingers (the strand under which you have just passed the loops). In one quick motion, begin opening fingers of left hand and with right hand bring string over left middle and ring fingers and

She looked at the four fine candles she had made.

straight up over the left palm. Do not pull too tightly or too weakly. This move takes a bit of practice.

Then she put them in the cupboard and left the room. Now, a thief had been looking in Grand-mother's window and saw where she put the candles.
"I need those candles," he said. He went in and stole them.

With right hand, drape top loop over left thumb. Let remaining strings fall gently down over left palm. To indicate theft, simply hold left hand gently in right hand, all strings intact, and move it quickly to one side.

19

When the thief got home he was tired from all the running, so he sat down

From above the back of the left hand (as pictured), place right index finger into loop on back of left middle finger; place right middle finger into loop on back of left ring finger.

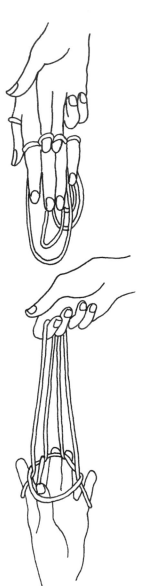

in his rocking chair. He was so tired he fell asleep while rocking. By the time he woke up, it was dark.

Holding the loops, pull right index and middle fingers up and forward in a smooth motion, while at the same time stretching the left thumb up and out and uncurling the left fingers. Tilt the "rocking chair" back and forth in rocking motions.

"I need one of those candles I stole," said the thief. "But first I must get my scissors."

He cut one of the candles off the bunch.

Allow left thumb loop to slide off and gently pull right index and middle fingers out until you have "scissors." Lift right index and lower right middle finger, then bring together again, in a scissoring motion. Repeat a few times.

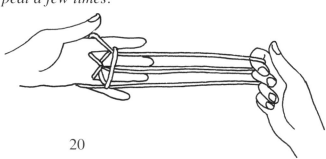

As he was cutting, a policeman passed by his window, looked in, and saw the bunch of candles. "Those must be the candles that Grandmother said were stolen from her cupboard," the policeman said. "I must go in and investigate."

He took out his billy club and knocked at the thief's door. "Open up in the name of the law!" The thief tried to hide the candles but before he could, the policeman was in the house. "You stole Grandmother's candles," he said. "There is the evidence. I am going to take you off to jail."
He got out his handcuffs, put them on the thief, and led him off to jail.

Keep on scissoring.

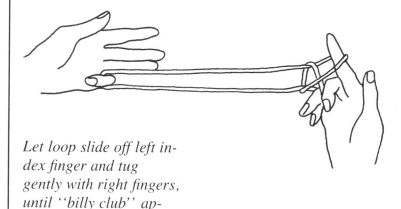

Let loop slide off left index finger and tug gently with right fingers, until "billy club" appears. Pretend to knock with "billy club," and then shake it, as though at the thief.

Continue to shake "billy club."

Let loop slide off right index finger. With left hand, move knot toward middle. Put both hands in "handcuffs."

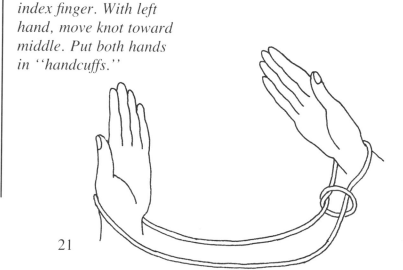

21

Lizard and Snake

For this story, I have combined three string tricks and put them together. The three-part story as given here is my invention. The first of the figures is known as "Lizard" in the Torres Straits, as "Eel" in the Marquesas, and as "Lizard and Snake" in parts of Papua New Guinea. The second has no special name given in C. F. Jayne or in any other source I can locate. The third is often called "the German trick" in Europe, and "The Palm" or "Lizard on a Palm Tree" in Papua New Guinea.

The first segment looks deceptively simple, but unless the hand is turned exactly as indicated, it will not work. This was a favorite string trick used by the early Hawaiians to win bets from strangers passing through. Though sure they could do the trick after seeing it once, strangers usually ended up with their hands caught in the string rather than free.

Recommended string length before knotting: 54 inches (135 cm)
Recommended strand length when braiding yarn: 65 inches (165 cm)

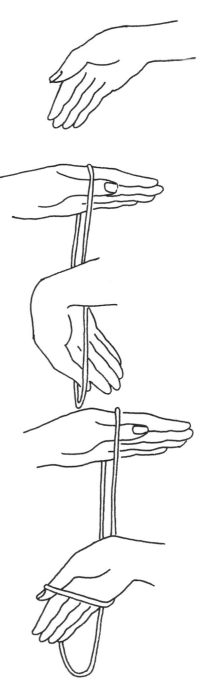

Prepare left hand by placing string over back of left thumb and fingers; hold left hand to one side.

Hold up right hand. Let it flop down loosely, as though it were Lizard settling on the rock.

Lizard liked nothing better than to sit on a rock in the hot sun. One day, Lizard found a nice flat stone and he went to stretch out in the warm sunshine, head down the way lizards like to lie. Even though his eyes were open, he was asleep. He did not see Snake creeping up closer and closer. "If I can get near enough, I shall swallow up Lizard and eat him, whole. He will make a fine morsel," thought Snake. Just then, Lizard woke up and tried to dart away, but too late! He was caught tight around his middle.

Bring left hand close to right hand, wiggling the string to imitate Snake. Move right hand downward, with palm facing away from body, then in a circular motion toward you and up.

While moving hand upward, bring middle part of front hanging strand up and over right hand. Try to do it in such a way that the string ends up tightly wound around right wrist.

23

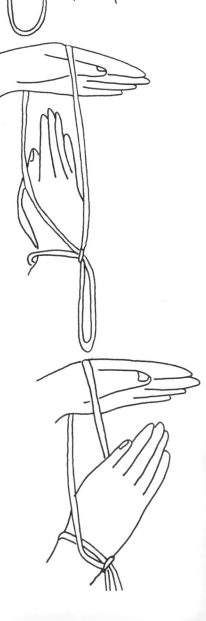

"Now I have you!" cried Snake. "I shall eat you up, and then have a long sleep."

"I must get out of here quickly," thought Lizard.

Now, lizards are very fast and tricky, and this one was no exception.

Point right hand straight up and move it to the side, so audience can clearly see that "Lizard" is caught tight.

"You don't have me yet, Snake," he said. He darted to the other side of Snake,

Move right hand to the left, completely around left side of outer string, until back of right hand is facing body.

slipped right through Snake's coils—

Bring right hand through loop and toward you.

24

and was gone!

Right hand is free.

A few days later, Lizard was again sunning himself on his rock. In fact, he was sound asleep. He had not seen Snake around for some time, so he felt quite safe.

But Snake was hungry again and he slithered up from behind. "This time I will wrap my tail tightly around Lizard's head and two front paws," said Snake.

Flop left hand loosely, fingertips downward. Keep right hand, with string, off to one side.

With right hand, bring string around to back of left hand and put it over left index and middle fingers, leaving the long loop hanging down behind left hand.

Snake wound his tail

Place right index finger under string in the space between left index and middle fingers.

down

and up and around Lizard's head and front paws.

At that moment Lizard awoke. "Oh, my!" he thought. "How can I get out of this?"

Curl tip of right index finger over back string and

pull it through until entire loop is hanging down front of palm.

Make sure loop is not twisted and that string wound around left index finger is hanging to the left; string wound around middle finger must be hanging to the right.

Put left thumb over left hanging string and under right hanging string.

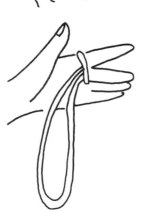

26

He put his back left paw under Snake to see if he could push Snake away from his front paws.

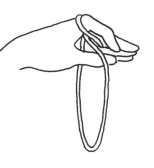

Bring left index finger forward to meet left thumb.

Snake saw what Lizard was trying to do. "I must wind myself around Lizard's *back* paws," he said. So he unwound one of his coils, getting ready to squeeze it around Lizard's hind legs.

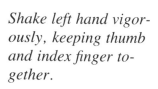

With right hand, lift loop off left middle finger and let it drop.

Lizard saw his chance. "Now I can get away," he said. He gave a flick of his tail

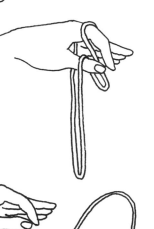

Shake left hand vigorously, keeping thumb and index finger together.

and left Snake lying there, wondering what had happened.

String will fall free.

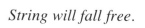

One day Lizard found a nest of eggs. He ate those eggs one after another until he could eat no more. Then, his belly swollen with food, he slowly climbed up on his rock to sit in the sun.

Flop left hand down. Keep string in right hand, off to one side.

This time when Snake came upon Lizard he said: "I am going to wind myself around his fat middle,

With right hand, wiggle string close to left hand and put string over it, leaving thumb free.

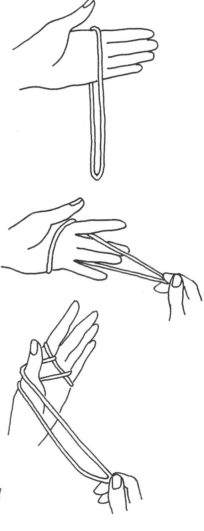

then around his front legs,

With right hand, pull the string forward from the back, so that the top strand is between index and middle fingers and bottom strand is between ring and little fingers.

then around his back legs,

Bring both strands around thumb, making sure that the top strand on thumb is the one that passed between index and middle fingers and the bottom strand on thumb is the one that passed between ring and little fingers.

then over his head,	*Move string to back of left hand again, making sure each strand goes back between the same fingers it was pulled through in the first place.*	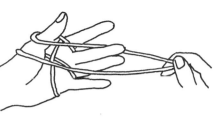
and around his front legs again.''	*Bring string back to front of left hand by looping upper strand around and over index finger and lower strand around and under little finger. Let string fall over front of left fingers.*	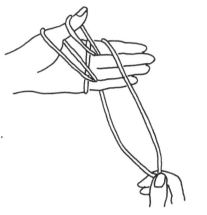
Lizard woke up and nodded his head. He shook his back paw.	*Wiggle left middle finger.* *Move left thumb.*	
"Caught again!" he thought. "Don't think you can get away this time," said Snake. "I will take these loose coils and wind them tightly around your neck.	*Take loops off thumb and pull them back tightly through space between left middle and ring fingers.*	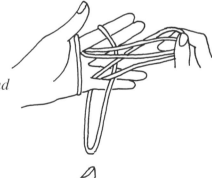
"Now I have you fast and tight."	*Close space tightly.*	

Out of the corner of his eye, Lizard saw his daughter. "Come quickly," he whispered. "I think if you pull Snake from around my middle he will come loose. It has been a long time since I ate those eggs, and now I am not so fat." Lizard's daughter poked her paw around Snake, right at the spot where he was wound tightly around Lizard's waist.

Curl right index finger under string running across left palm. (This may be done by a member of the audience; ask if someone in front row wishes to be Lizard's daughter.)

She gave a sharp pull— and Lizard was free! He and his daughter scuttled away to hide under the rocks. If you see Lizard some day, sitting on a rock and warming himself, watch closely and you may soon see Snake coming along.

*Pull sharply.
String falls free.*

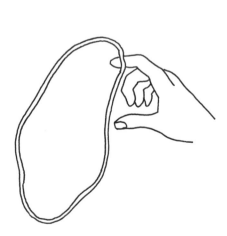

Cat's Cradle

This series of figures, requiring two players, is known throughout the world, although it is not necessarily done in the same sequence, nor does each stage have the same name in every language. No one knows for sure where "Cat's Cradle" began, or how it got its unusual names.

"Cat's Cradle" is ideally suited for spontaneous storytelling. The storyteller can compose a different tale each time, based on what images spring to mind at the moment of creation, or using the various names given to each figure by different peoples of the world. However, both players must know the figures well and agree on the sequence to be followed.

According to C. F. Jayne, the most commonly known names for the figures are:

1. Cradle   5. Diamond
2. Soldier's Bed   6. Cat's Eye
3. Candles   7. Fish in a Dish
4. Manger   8. Grandfather Clock

Here are two stories constructed around these names for the figures. The first is one that gradually evolved after many repetitions of string-figure performances I gave for individual children and groups. The second version is by a group of children.

Recommended string length before knotting: 60 inches (150 cm)
Recommended strand length when braiding yarn: 76 inches (188 cm)

Cat's Cradle—Version One

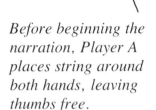

(No narration. In these instructions, Player A is referred to as female and Player B as male. Remember that in each case, the "near string" refers to the strand of string closest to the body of the person holding the string at the time. The "far string" is the strand farthest away from the body of the player holding the string at that moment.)

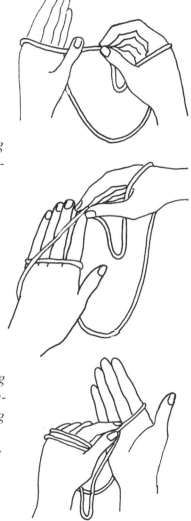

Before beginning the narration, Player A places string around both hands, leaving thumbs free.

With right thumb and index finger, Player A takes hold of near string and passes it around behind left hand,

so that it comes around all four fingers but not the thumb; there will now be two strands on back of left hand.

With left thumb and index finger, Player A takes hold of near string and passes it around behind right hand, leaving right thumb free. There will now be two strands around backs of both hands.

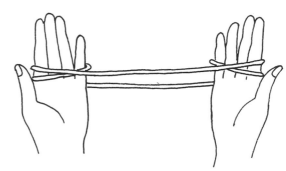

When Player A's hands are pulled apart, they will look like this.

There was once

Player A places tip of right middle finger under strand running across left palm; she leaves strand at approximately the first joint of right middle finger and pulls right hand back.

a little boy

Player A places tip of left middle finger under strand running across right palm; she leaves strand at approximately the first joint of left middle finger.

who slept in a cradle.

Player A pulls left hand back and separates hands until all strings are taut.

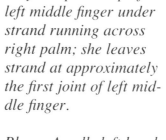

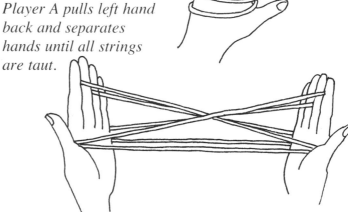

But it didn't take him long to grow up and when he became a young man he had to go off and serve in the army.

Then he slept . . .

Player B, standing to right of Player A, uses his left thumb and index finger to pick up the two near middle-finger strands where they cross. Then he uses his right thumb and index finger to pick up the two far middle-finger strands where they cross. Player B must be sure to have his left thumb and index finger pointing away *and his right thumb and index finger pointing toward Player A when starting this move. Player B separates his hands, drawing his right hand away from A and his left hand toward A, all the while pulling on strands.*

Player B pulls thumb and index finger of each hand, still holding strands, around corresponding side strands and up into center of figure. Player B then lifts his hands up, re-

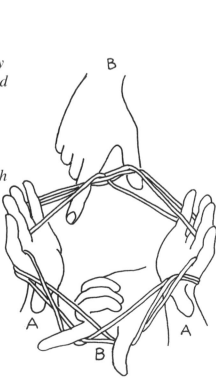

moving string from A's hands, and separates his index fingers from his thumbs.

A's hands leave the figure from below.

in a soldier's bed.

Player B extends his index fingers and thumbs until string is taut, to show the "soldier's bed."

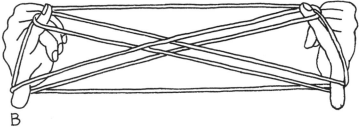

B

When his army duty had been completed, he set off for home . . .

Standing at right side of B, Player A now inserts her left index finger into B's left thumb loop and her left thumb into B's right thumb loop, near the center of the figure. She picks up the near *thumb strands where they cross. Player A then inserts her right thumb into B's right index loop and her right index finger into B's left index loop, and picks up the two* far *index finger strands where they cross.*

35

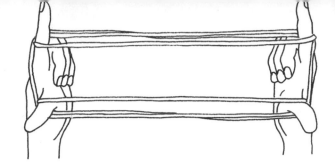

. . . with nothing in his pockets . . .

Player A separates her hands, drawing her right hand away *from B and over and past the far strand; her left hand draws the two strands to-ward B, over and past the near strand. A puts her thumbs and index fingers, still holding the strands,* under *the corresponding side strands and brings them up from below into the center of the figure. By lifting, drawing her hands apart, and separating her index fingers from her thumbs, she takes string from B's hands and forms the "candles and box."*

but two candles and a matchbox.

Player B, with his left hand palm up and fingers curled over, takes up the near index *strand in the bend of his left little finger and draws it over the near thumb strands toward A. Then, with his right palm up and fingers curled over, he takes up the* far thumb *strand in the bend of his right little finger and draws it over the far index strands away from A.*

He trudged along until it grew dark and then he stopped at a farmhouse to ask for a place to sleep.

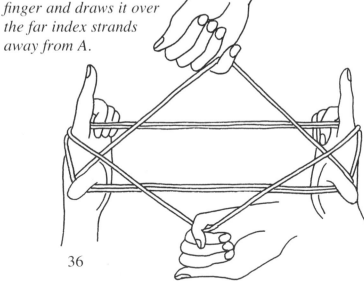

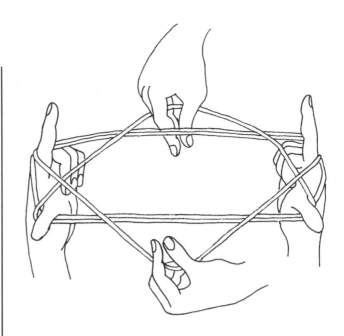

The farmer told the soldier he could sleep in the barn.

So that night the young man made his bed in a manger.

Closing the little fingers onto his palms, Player B puts his right thumb and index finger together and passes them, from the far side, under the two far index-finger strands; he places his left thumb and index finger together and passes them from the near side of A under the two near thumb strands. He moves both sets of index fingers and thumbs up into center of figure. Then Player B lifts up, taking string off A's hands, and draws his hands apart, separating index fingers and thumbs widely.

This forms the "manger."

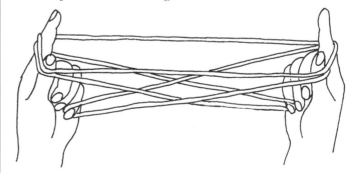

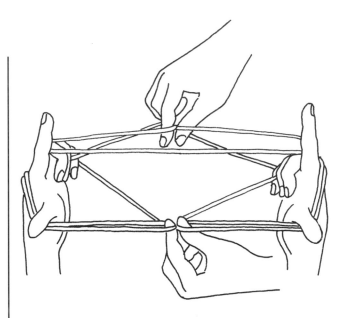

In the middle of the night, he heard a rustling noise. He lit one of his candles to see what was there. At first, he saw nothing, . . .

but then he noticed something shining up from under a clump of hay. He brushed away the hay and there sparkled a big diamond.

Player A now places her thumbs and index fingers over the crossed strands from below and prepares to take "manger" from B's hands in much the same way as B prepared to take "cradle" from her hands. However, this time A brings her thumbs and index fingers, holding the strands, up and over *the side strands and then* down into *the center of the figure.*

Player B takes his hands away from above.

When A draws her hands apart, thumbs and index fingers widely separated, she forms a figure similar to "soldier's bed," but in this case her thumbs and fingers are pointing downward.

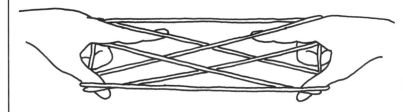

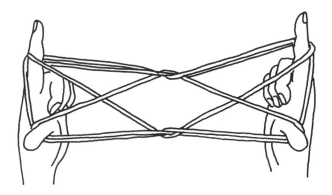

"Now I shall be rich," said the young man to himself. He reached over to pick up the diamond, when suddenly he heard the noise again. This time, when he looked up, peering at him was one glistening, ghostly cat's eye.

"I see what you have found," the eye seemed to be saying.

Player B now prepares to take the figure from A's hands in the same way A took "soldier's bed" from B, to form "candles and box." That is, B's right thumb and index finger go into A's index loops; his left thumb and index finger go into A's thumb loops; then he lifts thumbs and index fingers around the side strands and up from below into center of figure.

When B lifts up, removing string from A's hands, and separates his thumbs and index fingers widely, he forms the "cat's eye."

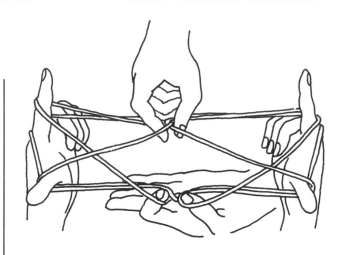

The young man stared back at the one-eyed cat. "Wait here," he whispered.

Player A now inserts her right index finger from above into far left triangle, her right thumb into far right triangle; she inserts her left index finger from above into near left triangle and her left thumb into near right triangle.

Before long he came back with—

Player A, still holding strands, turns her thumbs and index fingers straight toward each other, toward the center of the figure, but does not *bring them down into figure. B drops string and takes hands away from below.*

a fish in a dish.

Player A draws her hands apart and separates index fingers and thumbs widely, forming "fish in a dish."

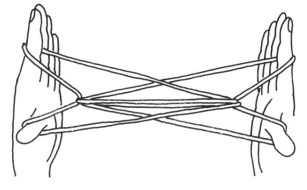

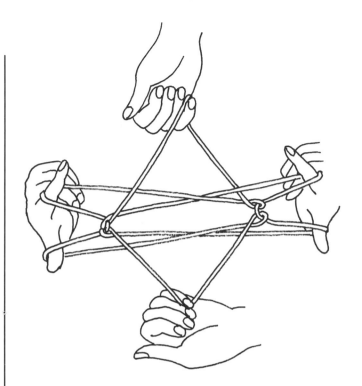

Then the young man picked up the diamond and put it into his pocket.

Player B now separates the two strands that pass from side to side through the center of the "fish." (If they do not separate easily into a near strand and a far strand without crossing each other exactly as in diagram, the last figure will not work out. It means that one player, at some point, either reversed the order of the steps, or stood at left side to take off string from other player. If this happens, begin again from start.) With palm facing up and fingers curled over, B picks up in bend of left little finger the near strand from inside of "fish"; he draws it over near thumb strands toward A. He then turns right hand so that palm is facing up and fingers are curled over. He picks up in bend of right little finger the far strand from inside of "fish"; he draws it over far index finger strands, away from A.

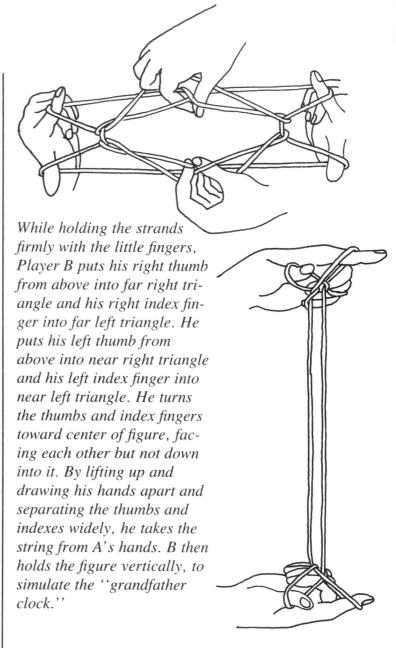

The next morning the soldier set off for his homeland again. The cat followed him.

"When I sell my diamond, I'll have enough for the two of us," said the young man, and he let the cat come with him.

The man spent the rest of his life sitting in his comfortable chair, listening to the ticktock of his grandfather clock and the contented purring of his one-eyed cat, who lay in the cradle the man had once slept in as a child. And that's why this story ended up being called "Cat's Cradle"!

While holding the strands firmly with the little fingers, Player B puts his right thumb from above into far right triangle and his right index finger into far left triangle. He puts his left thumb from above into near right triangle and his left index finger into near left triangle. He turns the thumbs and index fingers toward center of figure, facing each other but not down into it. By lifting up and drawing his hands apart and separating the thumbs and indexes widely, he takes the string from A's hands. B then holds the figure vertically, to simulate the "grandfather clock."

The moment A's hands are free, she takes a second string and makes the first figure of this story, the "cradle," and holds it up next to the "grandfather clock" that B is still holding up.

Cat's Cradle—Version Two:
Pembo

I frequently tell stories to groups of children in the United States and in other countries. Often my sessions end with a request for someone in the audience to come forward and share a story with me.

After I had told a number of string stories in the small town of Baldwin, Wisconsin, I was pleased to find that many of the children knew string patterns and had names for them, although they did not tell stories to accompany them. Emily and Molly Power and their friend Anna Rodel were particularly adept at the figures, so I asked them to compose their own version of the story behind the string pictures in the "Cat's Cradle" sequence. The result is this tale.

Once there was a baby named Pembo. He spent most of his time in his cradle. While she rocked him, Pembo's mother read aloud the letters that his father sent home from the war. Pembo felt sorry for Father, because he wrote that he had to sleep on a hard soldier's bed. When she had finished reading the letters, Mother sometimes sat by the fire and made candles. Pembo liked to watch as she put the finished candles neatly into a box.

Player A makes "cradle" as in Version One. Keep string high on middle fingers, so that "cradle" is narrower and taller than the "cradle" made by Player B in the fourth step, below.

Player A rocks "cradle" back and forth.

Player B takes string off as in Version One to make "soldier's bed."

Player A takes string off as in Version One to make "candles in box."

Months passed and suddenly—a surprise! Father came home, bringing many presents: a new, larger cradle for Pembo;

Player B takes string off as in Version One, to make second "cradle." This time, stretch fingers as far apart as possible.

a diamond for Mother;

Player A takes string off as in Version One to make the "diamond."

and a beautiful glass marble to play with during the long winter months. Shining up from deep inside the marble was a cat's eye.

Player B takes string off as in Version One to make the "cat's eye" figure.

That night, for their celebration dinner, they had Father's favorite—fish in a dish.

Player A takes string off as in Version One to make the "fish in a dish" figure.

After dinner, Father went outside to bring in his last surprise: a tall grandfather clock. And that was the gift Pembo and his mother liked best of all, because it was always there saying, "ticktock, ticktock."

Player B takes string off as in Version One to make the "grandfather clock."

String Stories—Bibliography

Ball, W. W. R. *String Figures*. London, 1921. Reprinted as *Fun with String Figures*. New York: Dover Publications, 1971.

Boas, Franz. "The Game of Cat's Cradle." *Internationales Archiv für Ethnographie,* Vol. 1 (1888), p. 229.

Cunnington, W. A. "String Figures and Tricks from Central Africa." *Journal of the Royal Anthropological Institute,* Vol. 36 (1906), pp. 121–131.

Dickey, Lyle Alexander. *String Figures from Hawaii, Including Some from New Hebrides and Gilbert Islands.* Bulletin 54. Honolulu: Bernice P. Bishop Museum, 1928.

Firth, Raymond, and Honor C. Maude. *Tikopia String Figures.* Occasional Paper No. 29. London: Royal Anthropological Institute, 1970.

Haddon, Kathleen. *Artists in String; String Figures: Their Regional Distribution and Social Significance.* London: Methuen, 1930.

Hingston, Margaret A. " 'The Candles' String Figure in Somerset." *Man,* Vol. 85, August 1903, p. 85; October 1903, p. 147.

Jayne, Caroline Furness. *String Figures and How to Make Them: A Study of Cat's-Cradle in Many Lands.* 1906. Reprint. New York: Dover Publications, 1962.

Koch, Gerd. *Fadenspiele.* 16-mm black-and-white films. Göttingen: Institut für den Wissenschaftlichen Film, n.d.

Leakey, M. D., and L. S. B. Leakey. *Some String Figures from Northeast Angola.* Lisbon, 1949.

Lutz, F. E. *String Figures from the Patomana Indians of British Guiana.* Anthropological Papers, Vol. 12. New York: American Museum of Natural History, 1912.

Maude, Honor C., and H. E. Maude. "String Figures from the Gilbert Islands." *Journal of the Polynesian Society,* Supplement, Memoir No. 13, pp. 1–72.

Parkinson, John. "Yoruba String Figures." *Journal of the Royal Anthropological Institute,* Vol. 36 (1906), pp. 132–141.

Sources of Additional Stories To Tell Using the String Method

Jayne's book (p. 45) has the best selection of string figures with key story words or phrases, as well as excellent instructions. By using the various titles of each figure and studying the folklore of the peoples concerned, one can invent expanded stories around the figures. Further, by going to the original sources cited in the Jayne bibliography, one can find additional bits and pieces of other versions to use in constructing the stories. The next best source, but more limited, is the book by W. W. R. Ball.

Cat's Cradle and Other String Figures by Joost Elffers and Michael Schuyt (Penguin, 1980) has a good selection of figures, but some of the instructions are very difficult to follow.

PART TWO

Picture-Drawing Stories

Picture-drawing stories or songs are not as widespread as string stories, yet they can be found in many countries. Simple cumulative tales, such as "The House That Jack Built," were frequently told and sketched out at the same time.

On a recent trip to Denmark, after I had sketched out examples of some American and Japanese picture-drawing stories, a Dane and an Icelander each chanted a story and drew a figure remarkably similar to the one in the Japanese "Number Story."

The most energetic picture-drawing storytellers are certain groups of indigenous Australians, among them the Walbiri and Ananda. These storytellers trace their pictures in sand, then erase them, only to draw the next symbols. These in turn will be erased or drawn over, on and on, in long cycles, until the teller gets tired and stops, sometimes in the middle of a story!

In the late nineteenth century and early years of the twentieth, various anthropologists and ethnologists reported that the Inuit (Eskimo) women and girls performed a similar kind of storytelling, in the snow in winter and in mud in summer. It was called storyknifing because they used a rounded knife made of whalebone to draw the pictures.

Picture-drawing stories are ideal for spur-of-the-moment storytelling, when a felt-tip pen and paper are handy. They also can provide comic relief when used in between longer, traditionally narrated stories.

The Black Cat

It is difficult to know whether this story became popular through folk telling or whether it spread as the result of Lewis Carroll's efforts. His version, called "Mr. T and Mr. C," was found among his diaries and other papers, and was surely used by him to entertain many of the children and adults with whom he socialized. It is reprinted at the end of Volume Two of his *Diaries*.

Two versions of this tale were reported in the *Journal of American Folklore* in 1897: one by Maud G. Early of Baltimore and the other by Ida Craddock of Philadelphia. Some years ago, the folklorist Carl Withers was inspired by these versions to write a picture book, *The Story of a Black Cat,* now out of print.

Recently, Paul Zelinsky illustrated *The Maid and the Mouse and the Odd-Shaped House,* a rhymed version found in the 1897 notebook of Jane Henriette Holzer, a schoolteacher in Bridgeport, Connecticut. Miss Holzer, it was reported, would have a different child go to the blackboard to add each additional part of the picture as the story unfolded.

The version given here combines the two variations of Early and Craddock; I have added a few details. When telling the story, I find it effective to cover the head portion of the cat with the non-drawing hand for the segment of the story when Tommy goes to Sally's house; then I lift it away at the moment of their arrival back at Tommy's house, when they see the big black cat.

This story is effective when drawn on a piece of paper for one, two, or three children; for larger groups, a blackboard or an overhead projector is better. Left-handed storytellers should draw the cat in the reverse of what is shown here.

There was once a boy named Tommy, and here's a T for Tommy. Tommy's best friend was Sally, who lived down the road in a dairy. And here's an S for Sally.

Tommy lived in a house with two rooms shaped like triangles. (Some versions prefer to make them square.)

In each room there was a window.

The house had two chimneys, one on each side of the roof.

To get in and out Tommy had a wee, double door. On both sides of the doorstep there were clumps of tall grass.

One day, Tommy came out of his house. He wanted to go and buy some cream from Sally. (Cover cat's head at this point.) He walked down the road until he came to Sally's house.

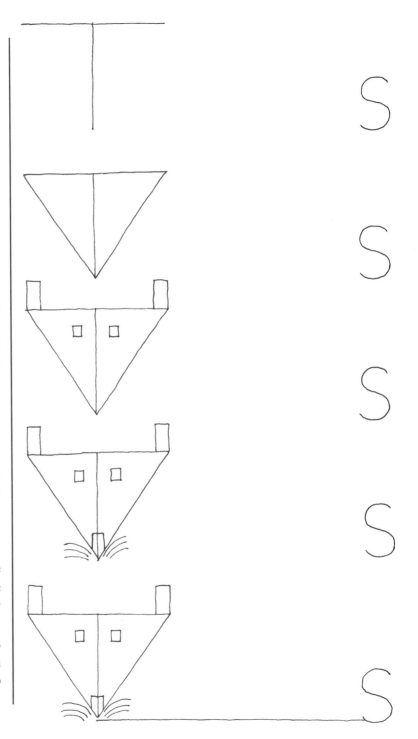

"I would like to buy some cream," said Tommy. "All right," said Sally. "Let's go into the cellar to get it." They went down to the cellar, (a) poured out a pitcherful of cream, and started to climb back up the steps. (b)

Tommy, who was carrying the pitcher, spilled some of the cream, and he and Sally slipped on it and tumbled back down into the cellar. (c)

"Let me carry it," said Sally. She took the pitcher and they climbed back up. (d)

When they got outside, Sally suggested they take the shortcut. They went along the path (e) for a while, but then, just before they were about to climb up the hill to Tommy's house, they came to a slippery spot and instead of climbing they fell down. (f) Up they jumped and as they were about to try climbing once (g) more, Sally spilled the cream and down she slid, with Tommy following after her. (h)

Free hand covers cat's head.

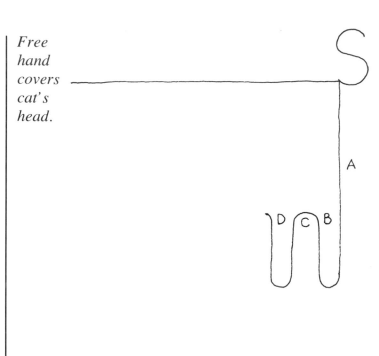

Free hand covers cat's head.

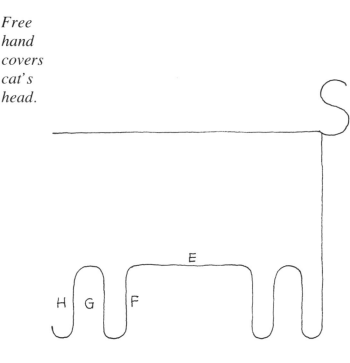

At last, carrying the empty pitcher, they were able to climb all the way up the hill to Tommy's house.(i)

"Oh!" cried Sally, "I wish I had some of the cream left."

"Why?" asked Tommy.

"For the big black cat!" (Lift hand from cat's head.)

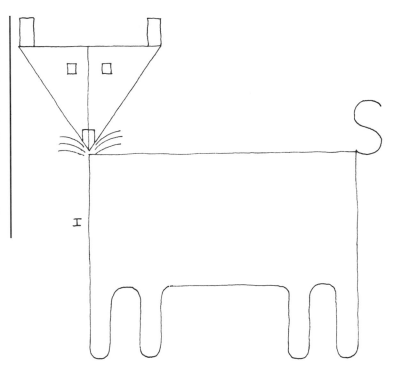

The Wild Bird

Different versions of this story were obviously widespread during the latter part of the nineteenth century and the early part of this century. In 1897, Ida Craddock reported on the version she remembered from her childhood. Laura Ingalls Wilder integrated a version told by her mother into "The Day of Games," a chapter of her book *On the Banks of Plum Creek*. In *Out of Africa*, the Danish writer Isak Dinesen reported still another variation that was told to her as a child, presumably by her European parents or nursemaids, although she does not say specifically who did the telling. The German writer Hans Baumann called attention to a variant found among the Mongolian peoples and published in *Mongolische Volksmärchen*.

The story as given here is basically the Craddock version, with a few changes suggested by other versions, and from many years of experience in telling the tale.

There was once an old man and his wife who lived in a round house.	*If left-handed, draw circle off to right, as here. If right-handed, make circle off to left.*	
The house had a smoke hole in the middle and a fenced-in backyard.	*Draw hole in circle and place "yard" at lower side. (Right-handers will place it on left side.)*	
Near the house was a large pond. Around the edges of the pond grew wild grasses and rushes.	*Draw oval pond, tilting it up slightly at one end. Make feathery strokes all around edge of pond.*	

In the middle of the pond there were always many fish swimming around.

One day, two hunters came to the pond to hunt and fish. They set up their tents to the south of the pond. That night the hunters were awakened by a strange, whirring noise.

"It's an animal of some kind," said the first hunter. "I'll go see what it is."

He left his tent and set off in the direction of the pond. It was dark and on the path was a stone. The hunter stumbled and made a terrible racket. He felt sure he had frightened away the animal. But when he got up, he still heard the whirring, so he continued walking in the direction of the pond.

Put feathery strokes in middle of pond, in wing position.

Place two tentlike figures below pond.

Draw line up middle of left tent, then angle it slightly toward left. Stop suddenly, make a circle to indicate stone. Then continue drawing line up, this time angling it slightly to right.

When he got there, what should he see but some fish flying out of one end of the pond. He became so engrossed in what he was seeing, he forgot about going back to tell his friend what was happening.

The second hunter waited in his tent and then could stand it no longer. He set off for the pond. But he, too, fell over a stone in the dark and then got up and continued on his way. When he arrived at the pond, he was so astonished by the flying fish, he forgot about scolding his friend.

Those fish kept coming out of the pond in long streaks, sailing out into the air. Now up in their little round house the man and his wife also heard the strange, whirring sounds. Finally, the man said, ''I must go and see what it is.''

Draw two or three fish leaping out of the pond.

Draw a line up through second tent and angle it slightly to the left. Stop suddenly, draw the round stone, and then continue at a slightly right angle, up to pond.

Draw three or four more flying fish.

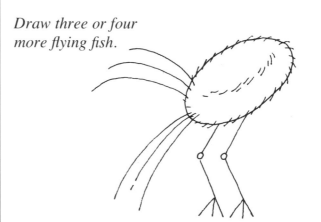

54

Off he went, running in a straight line for the pond. From the far side he could see those flying fish, sailing out into the air. He stood there, gaping, forgetting to go back and tell his wife.

The wife waited only a few minutes and then she set off. "Look," cried her husband the moment she arrived at the pond. "Look at the flying fish!" "What fish?" asked the wife. "All I see is a strange wild bird!"

Draw straight line from bottom of round house to pond.
Draw two or three more flying fish.
Keep drawing flying fish.

Draw second, parallel straight line from house to pond.

Bō ga Ippon
(What Will It Be?)

There are many picture-drawing story chants in Japan. Children usually start out with a dot, a line, a circle, or curve and then keep adding to complete the surprise picture. The chants are usually a series of three tones, re-fa-sol, which is characteristic of many Japanese folk melodies.

Some of these picture-drawing story chants are traditional and have been passed down for several generations. Others are composed spontaneously, either out of components used in other chants, or from new shapes and figures.

Here is one of the most commonly known picture-drawing story chants. I have changed the text in English slightly, to make it more understandable to non-Japanese children.

Once upon a time there was a stick.
No, not a stick, but a leaf.
No, not a leaf, but a frog.

No, not a frog, but a duck.

On the sixth of June, it rained like mad.

And a triangular ruler got a crack.

Balloons floated up all around.
Now let us go and see
The Monkey!

Bō ga ip - pon at - ta to - sa. Hap - pa ka - na,

Hap - pa ja na - i yo, ka - e - ru da - yo. Ka - e - ru ja

na - i yo, A - hi - ru da - yo. Ro - ku ga - tsu mu - i - ka ni

a - me zā - zā fut - te ki - te, San - ka - ku jo - gi ni

hi - bi it - te, Kop - pe - pa - n fu - ta - tsu, ma - me mit -

tsu, a - n - pa - n fu - ta - tsu ku - da - sa - i na.

At - to yu ma ni ka - wa - i - i kok - ku sa - n.

57

Number Story

The figures for this Japanese picture-drawing chant can be found in several journals and folklore collections in Japanese, but the words differ and are often so sketchy that they do not make sense at all to the non-Japanese person. I have invented my own text, using a few elements from some of the versions, but essentially constructing a new story.

The rhythm and musical pattern of the chant are similar to "Bō ga Ippon." Therefore, rather than a straightforward, narrative voice, use a rhythmic, chanting voice. To be effective, this must be told smoothly and quickly.

Once there was a Big Six who had two children: right-handed Little Six and left-handed Little Six.	*Draw a large 6 (a).* *Draw a smaller 6, below, to the left (b); then draw a backward 6 (ð) to the right (c). Remember to make these the* opposite *of what you are saying.*
Their friend was Lazy Eight, who lived down the street.	*Draw an 8 below, on its side (d). Be sure to leave space between the small sixes and the eight.*

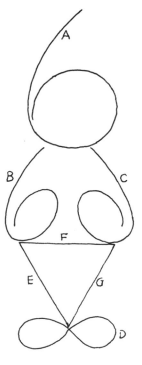

58

One day Lazy Eight went to right-handed Little Six to borrow a triangular ruler.

"Go to left-handed Little Six; he has it, not I."

"Here it is," said left-handed Little Six.

Lazy Eight took the triangular ruler home.

But as soon as he got it there, he dropped it and it cracked.

The zeros floated up,
all
ten
of them.

"I am nothing but a dunce!" Lazy Eight said. And he was!

Draw line from middle of ∞ to bottom of 6 on left (e).

Draw line from 6 on left to ð on right (f).

Draw line from ð on right, back down to middle of ∞ (g).

Draw line up middle of triangle (h).

Put three zeros in like buttons (i),
three like a mouth (j),
one for a nose (k),
two for eyes (l),
and one for the
tip of the hat (m).

Make the stroke for ten (to complete the hat, n) and lift away both hands.

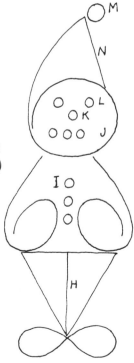

Sand Stories

One of the most unusual forms of picture-drawing stories is that practiced by the Walbiri, the Ananda, and other peoples indigenous to Australia. I first learned about sand storytelling from Jack Davis, an aboriginal folklorist who spoke at a conference I attended in Sydney (see the item under his name in the bibliography at the end of this section). His description intrigued me so much, I began to search for other information on sand storytelling and then found Nancy Munn's excellent book *Walbiri Iconography*. It gives a very complete description of the methods and meaning of this type of storytelling.

I later studied bark paintings and other books related to aboriginal art and writing. From all this information, I adapted the symbols to suit the stories I selected and then began telling them on the homemade sand screen I had devised for use on the overhead projector.

This form of storytelling is practiced mostly by women and girls. The teller selects a space in the sand about a foot or two in diameter, clears it of sticks, stones, and other debris, and begins narrating the story in a singsong style, while at the same time drawing the graphic designs in the sand. Gestures are also used.

When telling this kind of story at the beach or a camp, use the sand readily available on the ground. Some schools or institutions have sand tables in play areas, and a sand storytelling event could be imitated by sitting around such a sand table.

However, the easiest method is to use the sand screen on the overhead projector. Directions to make such a screen are given on pages 61–62. I carry the sand in a glass jar or plastic bag and pour it out just before beginning the story. You will need to experiment to get exactly the right amount in order to have the sand flow properly when making the designs and shaking the screen.

The stark quality of the black-and-white figures, and the fleeting quality of the images, seem to me to be remarkably similar to those that would appear in a sand story drawn on the ground.

Instructions for Making and Using a Sandbox
for Showing Sand Stories on an Overhead Projector

Materials needed:

1 shallow but sturdy box or box cover, approximately 10 inches by
12 inches (25 cm by 30 cm) (no deeper than 2 inches or 6 cm)

1 piece heavy, clear acetate, 9 inches by 10 inches (22 cm by 25
cm)

or glass of same size

or plexiglass of same size

(Glass definitely works the best since the sand does not scratch it;
however, acetate is the lightest and least susceptible to breakage.)

Cloth tape or strong masking tape

1 large plastic comb, 8-inch (20-cm) size

½ to 1 cup fine sand (The ordinary kind used on construction proj-
ects is fine if you sift it through a tea strainer.)

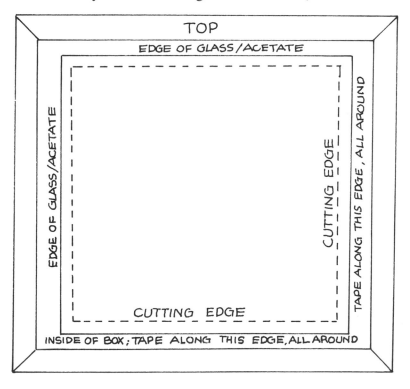

Measure and mark the lines of an opening to be cut in the box bottom; the opening should be ⅜ inch (1 cm) *smaller* than the acetate or glass *on all four sides*. (See diagram on page 61.)

Using a sharp artist's knife or razor in a holder, very carefully cut out the opening.

Place acetate or glass over opening and tape down *on the inside* of box, making sure all edges are smooth.

Mark one of the slightly longer edges "top."

When telling the stories, make sure the edge marked "top" is placed on the plate of the overhead projector in such a way that it shows up on the top of the screen, where the image is projected.

To smooth the sand and ready it for the next pictures, shake the box from side to side, or use the comb, or both. With practice, you will soon get the feel of just how thick to make the layer of sand, and how best to smooth it out.

Use the index finger of one hand to draw the pictures, starting at the top whenever possible, and moving downward.

If you wish, before beginning the story, introduce some of the pictures that will appear in the sand story and tell the audience what they stand for, as indicated below.* However, I often tell the stories without first doing the pictures, and it is equally effective.

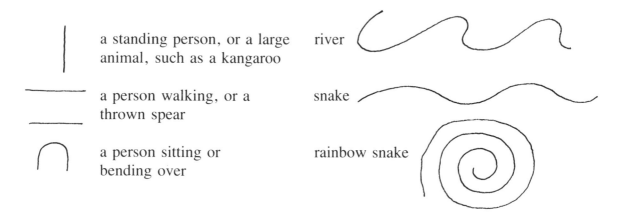

a standing person, or a large animal, such as a kangaroo	river	
a person walking, or a thrown spear	snake	
a person sitting or bending over	rainbow snake	

*Adapted from figures in Munn, *Walbiri Iconography*, and from bark and rock paintings found in Australia.

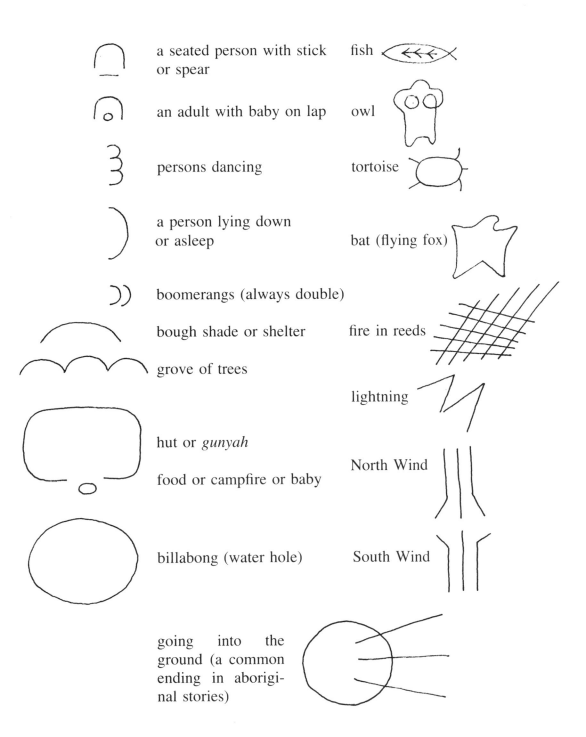

a seated person with stick or spear	fish
an adult with baby on lap	owl
persons dancing	tortoise
a person lying down or asleep	bat (flying fox)
boomerangs (always double)	
bough shade or shelter	fire in reeds
grove of trees	
	lightning
hut or *gunyah*	
food or campfire or baby	North Wind
billabong (water hole)	South Wind
going into the ground (a common ending in aboriginal stories)	

The Rainbow Snake

(adapted from a version recorded by Roland Robinson)

In the Dreaming, old man Nagacork made a deep billabong, a water hole, in the Flying Fox River.

Nagacork went on a long walkabout, and when he returned to the billabong, he saw the smoke of many campfires rising through the pandanus palms and the paperbark trees.

As he came nearer, he heard the talking and laughing of many tribesmen sitting under the shady trees.

Along the riverbank he saw the tribesmen spearing for fish.

He saw the women and children wading among the lilies and feeling with their hands and feet in the deep mud for the lily buds and the mussels. They were singing and calling to one another.

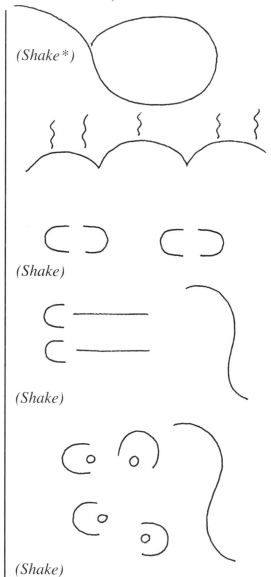

(Shake*)

(Shake)

(Shake)

(Shake)

*Whenever the word "Shake" is used, smooth out the sand either by shaking it or combing it and start with a fresh design.

When the tribesmen saw Nagacork they called out to him, "Come on, old man, there are plenty of fish here." But old man Nagacork went on under the trees along the riverbank. Parties of tribesmen going from camp to camp passed him as he went along.

Nagacork was looking for Jammutt, his water-shooting fish. He had not seen Jammutt in any part of the river. As he walked along, looking, the tribesmen along the banks pointed with their spears and called out, "Here, old man! Are these the fish you are looking for?"

"No," said Nagacork. "They are not my Jammutt, my water-shooting fish. It does not matter. I'll go to my camp." And as Nagacork turned to go he saw a stream of ants passing over the ground and going up a big collibah tree. The ants crawled higher and higher until they disappeared into a hole at the top of the tree.

Nagacork climbed up the tree and looked into the hole. In the darkness he saw the bones of Jammutt, his lost water-shooting fish. The tribesmen had killed and eaten Jammutt and hidden the bones.

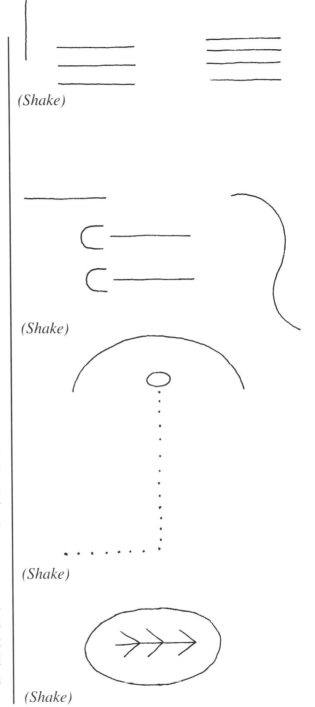

(Shake)

(Shake)

(Shake)

(Shake)

65

Old man Nagacork climbed down and went to his camp under a clump of pandanus palms. He sat with his head on his arms across his knees, thinking about his lost water-shooting fish. And as he sat he began to sing to himself: "I wait, wait, wait, wait, wait. I wait, wait, wait, wait, wait."

Suddenly it seemed to him that he was singing up Kurrichalpongo, the black rock snake. High up in the paperbark trees, Dat-Dat, the green parrot, began to call out that he could see the great rock snake coming out of the mountains in the north.

And then, high in the sky, far above the tops of the trees, old man Nagacork saw the wide curve of the rainbow appear.

(Shake)

Kurrichalpongo, the rock snake, went under the ground and bored a hole in the bank of the billabong, and let in a rush of water. As the tribesmen were swimming and wading, they suddenly saw the water rising.
At first the water was up to their thighs.

66

Then it was up to their chests. The water rose and covered the reeds and lilies.

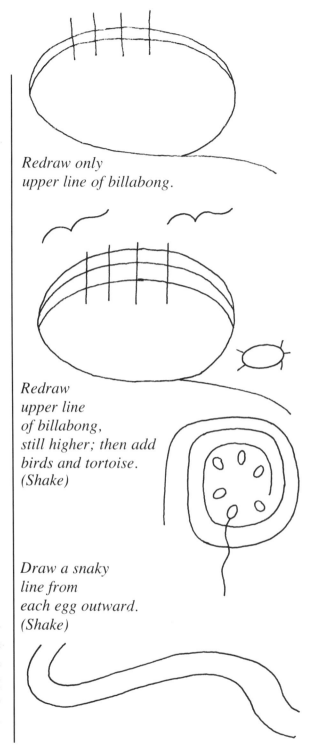

*Redraw only
upper line of billabong.*

It rose and spread over the banks, flooding the camps of the tribesmen. Many were drowned as it rose.
But some tribesmen changed themselves into birds and flew up and away. Others, to escape being drowned, changed into tortoises.

*Redraw
upper line
of billabong,
still higher; then add
birds and tortoise.
(Shake)*

Kurrichalpongo, the black rock snake, laid many eggs at this place. And when the eggs hatched out, they were young rainbow snakes.
The young rainbow snakes started to travel in many directions.

*Draw a snaky
line from
each egg outward.
(Shake)*

But Kurrichalpongo went on to Yoo-loo, on the Wilton River. And as the black rock snake went along, she looked back and saw that the winding track she was making was turning into a deep, wide river with trees and reeds and lilies.

"What is happening?" asked Kurri-chalpongo. "How am I doing this?" Then, on the plain, Kurrichalpongo met and fought the dingo, the wild dog. After she had vanquished him, she lay down to rest and upon rising, saw that she had created the bitter yams that grow there.

Traveling on, Kurrichalpongo made a big swamp. On and on she went until she came to Luralingi.

Now, at Luralingi there lived two young men, sons of Nagacork. They had found two of the small rainbow snakes—one in a tree and one in a cave nearby—and they killed them. The two young men took the dead snakes to their father, Nagacork. "Look what we have brought for food," they said.

Nagacork frowned when he saw the snakes. "You should not have done that," he said. "Those are rainbow snakes you have killed. You will surely die for doing that."

And it was then that Kurrichalpongo arrived at Luralingi. In her anger at what the two young men had done, she turned into Bolong, the rainbow snake, and as she did so, lightning with many tongues forked out into the sky, and thunder came with the noise of mountains being split apart.

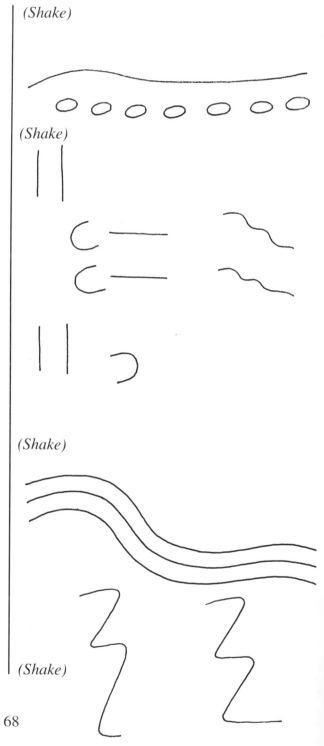

(Shake)

(Shake)

(Shake)

(Shake)

68

The rain and the wind came, snapping off and uprooting trees. And the mountains fell down on the tribes and the water came, swirling trees and tribesmen as it rushed along.

Many were the tribes that were drowned then.

At last, Bolong, the rainbow snake, changed herself back into Kurrichalpongo.

She traveled then to Moorinjairee, which in English is called Newcastle Waters. There she met old man Nagacork and four rainbow snakes. They made a corroboree.

And at this place called Moorinjairee, where there are hundreds of billabongs, the Dreaming ended.
The animals who turned into tribesmen have remained as humans ever since, and those tribesmen who changed into animals have kept their animal form. And Kurrichalpongo and the rainbow snakes went down into the ground.

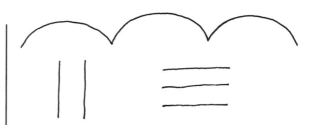

Swirl with the fingers, then shake.

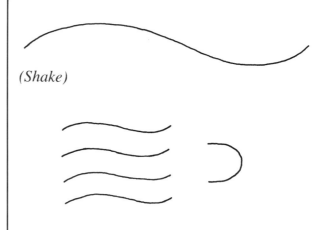

(Shake)

(Shake)

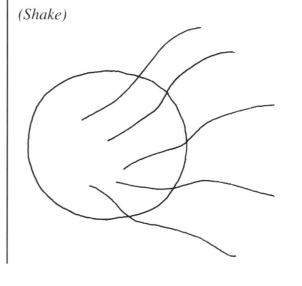

Why There Is Fire in Wood

This is adapted from a story collected by K. Langloh Parker, published in *Woggheeguy* (see bibliography at end of this section).

Goodoo, the Codfish,[1] was a great wizard and it was he who first made fires. It was said he had once caught a flash of lightning[2] and imprisoned it for his own use.

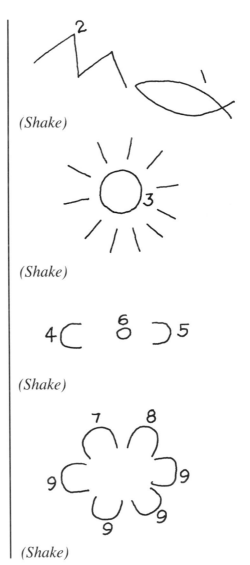

(Shake)

After that, instead of waiting for the sun[3] to dry his food, he used fire to cook it.

For a long time he kept his secret.

But Goodoo was really very lazy[4] and didn't like to do his cooking. He told his secret to Goomai, the Water Rat,[5] on condition that Goomai do the cooking.

(Shake)

Goomai was glad to do it.[6] He preferred fire-cooked food to the raw or sun-dried meat he usually had to eat. Moreover, when the Sun went to bed, it was very pleasant to have a fire to stay warm. The rest of the tribes[7] were jealous. They asked to be in on the secret,[8] but Goodoo and Goomai would not share it. They called a big corroboree[9] to discuss the situation. It was decided they would try to get hold of the secret of fire, even if they must steal it.

(Shake)

(Shake)

70

"Surely," said Narahdarn [10] the Bat, "the whole of us are good enough to outwit those two."

There was much talk, first of one idea,[11] then another.[12] At last, Mullyan,[13] the great Eagle Hawk, rose up and told them to cease chattering.

"Leave it to me," he said. "I'll get fire for you."

And, as Mullyan was noted for his wisdom and strength, it was decided to leave it to him.

The next day, Goodoo [14] and Goomai [15] went to gather mussels at the water's edge.[16] When they had a dilly bag full of them, they [17] cleared a space in the reeds,[18] made their fire,[19] and started to cook the mussels.

Mullyan flew over them on high,[20] chuckling to himself.

He called on his relative, the North Wind,[21] to blow the fire toward the reeds until they caught fire.

The North Wind blew and blew [22] until the reeds caught fire.[23]

But Goodoo and Goomai threw water on them and stopped the fire from spreading.

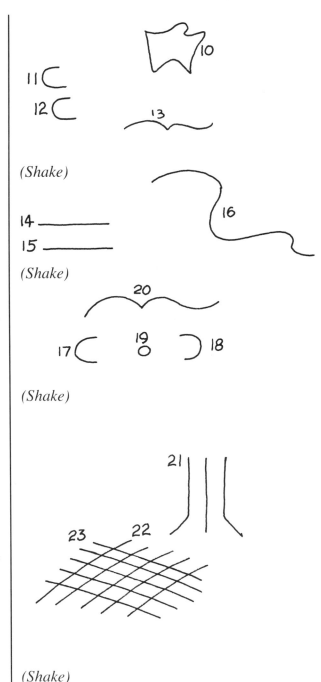

(Shake)

(Shake)

(Shake)

(Shake)

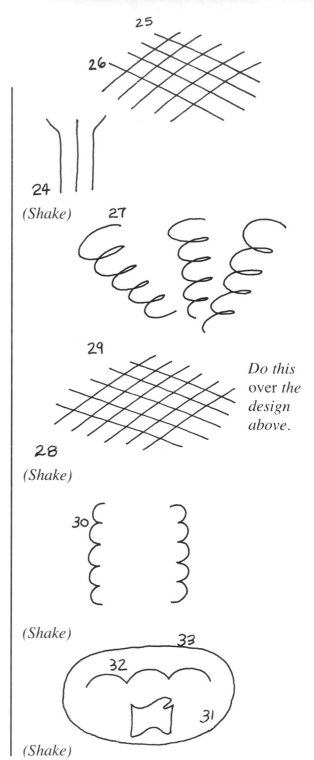

Then Mullyan called on the South Wind,[24] and the South Wind blew and blew[25] until the reeds on the other side caught fire.[26] But once again Goodoo and Goomai put out the flames.

But Mullyan would not be beaten. So he sent Wurrawilberoo, a devil in a whirlwind,[27] and that caught up the fire and blew the coals in all directions.

The fire raced through the reeds,[28] leaping and flaming with forked tongues in all directions.[29] Goodoo and Goomai could not keep it from spreading.

The tribes were delighted and danced[30] before the burning reeds.

But Narahdarn, the Bat,[31] did not join them. He ran to a grove of trees[32] and burned a ring around them[33] to save them from being destroyed. A few tribesmen saw him as he slipped coals of fire into the bark of some of the trees.

24
(Shake)

25
26

27

Do this over the design above.

29

28
(Shake)

30

(Shake)

32
33
31

(Shake)

72

The tribesmen laughed,[34] but Narahdarn[35] answered, "Wait a while. You will soon be glad I knew what to do."

That was all he would say, so the tribesmen went on with their dancing,[36] and some cooked food over a fire.[37]

When Goodoo[38] and Goomai[39] saw that the fire had escaped them, they talked about what they should do. Goodoo, being a wizard, was also a rainmaker, so he began to sing his rain song.[40] He went to the river[41] and threw in his magic rain pebbles,[42] as well as a few branches from the sacred tree.[43] While he was doing this, Goomai[44] was building a raised-up *gunyah*.[45] Every now and then he would look over to the dancing tribesmen and shake his head, saying, "Poor fools![46] Their time is nearly up. Can't they see the rain clouds forming? No, they're too busy dancing![47] Poor fools!"

As soon as the *gunyah*[48] was finished, Goodoo[49] and Goomai[50] put all their possessions in it,[51] together with all the food they had.

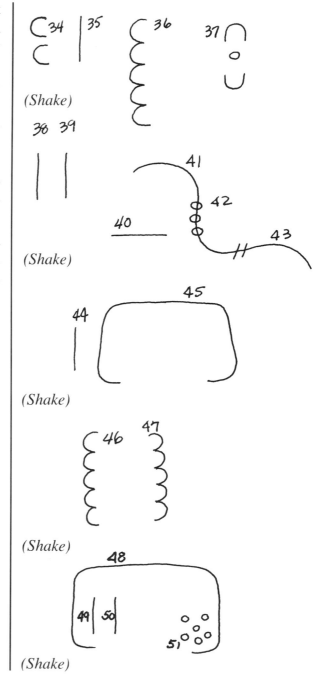

(Shake)

(Shake)

(Shake)

(Shake)

(Shake)

73

Soon the clouds burst. Never had the world seen such a flood.[52] It poured for days and days. The tribesmen[53] rushed about for shelter, but too late! Narahdarn[54] came to Goodoo[55] and begged to be saved.[56] Goodoo would not listen at first. "But I have a secret," said Narahdarn. "If you save me and my women relatives, especially my little sister Boolooral, the Owl, I will tell you how you can still find fire after the flood goes down."

When Goodoo[57] heard Narahdarn's secret[58] he let the Bat come in[59] but he refused to let in Owl and the other women relatives. But Boolooral cried so piteously that Goodoo took pity on her and let them all come in the *gunyah*.[60]

When the earth was dry again, Narahdarn[61] flew to one of the trees[62] in which he had placed coals. He brought back two sticks[63] and showed Goodoo[64] how to rub them together to make fire, any time he wanted it. And ever since that time the men of the tribes honor Narahdarn[65] for saving their kind, and the women honor his little sister, Owl,[66] for saving theirs.

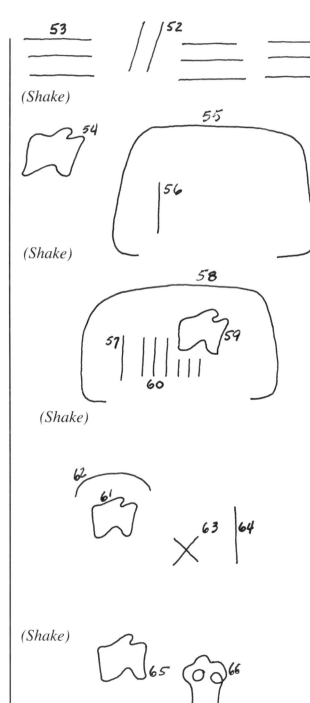

(Shake)

(Shake)

(Shake)

(Shake)

74

Picture-Drawing Stories—Bibliography

Sand Stories

Allen, Louise A. *Time Before Morning: Art and Myth of the Australian Aborigines.* New York: T. Y. Crowell, 1975.

Berndt, Ronald M., and Catherine H. Berndt. *The World of the First Australians.* Sydney: Ure Smith, 1965.

Berndt, Catherine H. "The Rainbow Serpent Lives." In *Through Folklore to Literature,* edited by Maurice Saxby, pp. 133–150. Sydney: IBBY Australia (P.O. Box 194, Edgecliff, NSW 2027, Australia), 1979.

Davis, Jack. "Story Traditions in Australian Aboriginal Cultures." In *Through Folklore to Literature,* edited by Maurice Saxby, pp. 121–132. Sydney: IBBY Australia (see above), 1979.

Elkin, Adolphus P., and Catherine and Ronald Berndt. *Art in Arnheim Land.* Chicago: University of Chicago Press, 1950.

Munn, Nancy D. *Walbiri Iconography.* Ithaca, N.Y.: Cornell University Press, 1973.

Parker, K. Langloh. *Australian Legendary Tales.* New York: Viking, 1966.

———. *Woggheeguy: Australian Aboriginal Legends.* Adelaide: F. W. Preece, 1930.

Robinson, Roland. *The Feathered Serpent.* Sydney: Edwards and Shaw, 1956.

———. *Legend and Dreaming.* Sydney: Edwards and Shaw, 1952.

Ucko, Peter J. *Form in Indigenous Art.* Prehistory and Material Culture Series, 13. Canberra: Australian Institute of Aboriginal Studies, 1977.

Wallace, Phyl, and Noel Wallace. "Milpatjunanyi, the Story Game." In *Children of the Desert,* pp. 24–26. Melbourne: Thomas Nelson, 1968.

Japanese

"Bō ga Ippon." In *Folk and Traditional Music of Asia for Children,* Vol. 1. LP disc and booklet. Tokyo: Asian Cultural Center for UNESCO, 1975.

Kako, Satoshi. *Nihon Denshō No Asobi Tokumon* [Japanese collection of traditional games]. Tokyo: Fukuinkan Shoten, 1967.

American, European, and Asian

Baumann, Hans. "Der Wolf und die Ziegen." In personal letter to the author, April 1983.

Craddock, Ida C. "The Black Cat" and "The Wild Fowl." *Journal of American Folklore,* 1897, pp. 322–323.

Dinesen, Isak. *Out of Africa.* New York: Random House, 1938, p. 251.

Dodgson, Charles Lutwidge. "Mr. T. and Mr. C." In *The Diaries of Lewis Carroll,* edited by Roger Lancelyn Green, Vol. 2, Appendix. New York: Oxford University Press, 1954.

Heissig, Walter, trans. and ed. *Mongolische Volksmärchen.* Düsseldorf: E. Diedrichs, 1963, pp. 125–129.

Early, Maud G. "The Tale of the Wild Cat." *Journal of American Folklore,* 1897, p. 80.

Withers, Carl. *The Tale of a Black Cat.* Illustrated by Alan Cober. New York: Holt, Rinehart, 1966.

Zelinsky, Paul. *The Maid and the Mouse and the Odd-Shaped House.* New York: Dodd, Mead, 1981.

PART THREE

Stories with Dolls
or Figurines

When traveling around the world, one often comes upon unusual dolls, figures, or objects. Sometimes these are relatively unknown outside their native country. In other cases, they have become tourist souvenirs that one can also find in import and gift stores in North America and Europe. However, they often retain enough of their folk imprint to suggest they had, or still have, stories attached to them.

This section deals with exactly such items and the stories behind them.

Not every attractive souvenir will have folk authenticity behind it, so the storyteller should select wisely and do some preliminary research before attempting to unearth an object's story. However, when properly backed up with information on the history and/or legend associated with the object, this kind of storytelling is immensely rewarding. It offers the chance to introduce bits and pieces of other cultures in an attractive, intriguing way.

Though purists might contend this is no way to introduce the complexities of another culture, research at the Information Center on Children's Cultures shows that when such popular and pleasing artifacts are used, the listeners are more inclined to respond later to the more subtle and challenging distinctions of that other culture.

Nesting Dolls
(Matrioska)

This kind of doll appears to be about one hundred years old. Some specialists in the history of toys speculate that it was inspired by the beautiful, handcrafted sets of Japanese nesting boxes that began to appear in Europe in the nineteenth century.

Two early histories of Russian toys make no mention of the *matrioska,* yet the Toy Museum in Zagorsk has several sets that have been dated to the late nineteenth century. There are also Czech, Polish, and German sets that date to the turn of the century.

Max von Boehn states, in *Puppen und Puppenspiele,* that the nesting doll originated in the studios of the wooden toy makers in and around Munich. Photographs in his book show nesting dolls of peasant women from the first decade of this century that look much more Germanic than the Slavic types we are accustomed to seeing today. Boehn believed the dolls did not "catch on" in the commercial European market because they made a "greater appeal to the grown-ups than to children."

It seems likely to me that the *matrioska* dolls did catch on in the Slavic countries for several reasons. One logical reason could be the prevalence of the Marzanna customs, even up to the present day, in certain rural areas of the Slavic countries. Marzanna was an old grandmother figure, a kind of goddess of death. In certain villages, a straw or wooden effigy of Marzanna was constructed at the end of winter and then taken by a group of young people to the river and thrown in, so that it would float away. Alternatively, it might be burned in the fields. Upon their return from "carrying away death," the young people, often only the girls, brought back into the village a tree sprout with a doll hanging in it. Sometimes the doll was hidden inside the Marzanna effigy and taken out before the effigy was dispatched, reenacting a kind of resurrection, a life out of death.

Another reason for the survival of the *matrioska* dolls in the Slavic countries is possibly the fact that the grandmother figure is very common in the folktales in that part of Europe. A doll representing several generations, with the largest (and thus most respected) being the grandmother or great-grandmother, would have an immediate impact on people who could attach the dolls to the folktales of the area.

Whatever the reasons, it was only in Russia, Poland, Czechoslovakia, and a few other parts of central Europe that the nesting dolls continued to be made by craft workers. Few of the dolls left the region, because they were not produced in enough quantity for export sale.

Then, for the World's Fair Exhibition at Brussels in 1958, the Russians hit on the idea of the *matrioska* as a symbol and captured the imagination of most visitors to the fair with their attractive display of nesting dolls in all shapes and sizes. From that moment on, the *matrioska* began to be produced as a tourist item as well as for its folkloric qualities.

I have seen a number of storytellers effectively use the *matrioska* doll to introduce stories from the Slavic countries by saying something like this: "My great-grandmother told this story to my grandmother who told it to my mother and she told it to me." For each generation, the storyteller opens up the doll set and shows the next doll inside.

When visiting Russia and Poland, I occasionally saw sets of nesting dolls used in kindergartens to accompany spontaneous stories that appeared to be partially adapted from cautionary tales taken from folkloric sources. The stories usually involved grandmothers or mothers who had many children.

"Marysia" is a story I made up after hearing a similar one told in a Warsaw kindergarten many years ago. The actions, as much as the tale, were used to educate as well as entertain. They were intended to help teach the children size and spatial relationships.

I find that this story works well on both levels: as entertainment and as an educational device. There is something irresistible about taking apart and putting together again the sets of dolls in their graduated sizes. For best results, use a set of dolls ranging from medium size to very small size. The tinier the inmost doll is, the better.

Naughty Marysia

There was once a little girl named Marysia. (That means ''little Mary'' in Polish.) Marysia had a great-grandmother, a grandmother, a mother, an older sister, and a baby sister. She also had (. . . and)* a father but he was out in the fields working.

Marysia's mother said to her: ''I want you to take Baby Sister outside and play with her. But do not leave the front yard.''

Marysia took Baby Sister by the hand and they went out. They played together for a while. But suddenly Marysia felt mischievous. ''I am going to take Baby Sister and hide,'' she said. And she did. Soon, Great-Grandmother came out to check on Marysia and Baby Sister. She looked all around the yard but she saw no sign of them.

Hold doll set cupped in hands, unseen by audience.

Hold doll set out in right hand. Move it about, pretending to look in all corners.

*If your set has more than six dolls, add characters to match.

"That naughty girl. I think she has taken Baby Sister off to the woods. They are sure to get lost. I had better go and find them." So Great-Grandmother went off to the woods.

When Great-Grandmother did not return, Grandmother went out to look. "Where can that naughty Marysia have gone?" she asked. She looked off to the left. "I think she must have gone off to play with Baby Sister by the river. That is dangerous. They are sure to fall in. I shall have to go and get them." So Grandmother went off to the river.

After a bit, when neither Great-Grandmother nor Grandmother came back, Mother went out to investigate.
"Where have they all gone?" she wondered. "Especially that naughty Marysia who was supposed to stay here watching Baby Sister. I

Take outer doll apart, leave rest of set hidden in left hand, and with right hand put Great-Grandmother doll (outer doll) in some spot off to right.

Move doll set around as though looking in all corners.

Take next doll (second largest) apart, but keep rest of set hidden in left hand. Put Grandmother down at some appropriate spot off to left.

Move doll set around as though looking in all corners.

81

know, I think they must have gone off to the fields where Father is working. They are not supposed to be pestering him. I'll go and bring them back.''

So Mother went off to the fields. (Aunt Anna might go to the barn; Cousin Katherine might go to the garden, etc.)

When Great-Grand-mother, Grandmother, and Mother did not re-turn, Older Sister came out. ''Where have those sisters of mine gone?'' she wondered. She looked all around and could not see them. ''I think they must have gone to the village to get some candy or sweets, and I want some, too!''

So Older Sister went off to the village.

As soon as Older Sister had gone off, Marysia stepped out from where she had been hiding.

Take next doll (third largest) apart, but keep rest of set hidden in left hand. Put Mother down in spot selected to rep-resent fields.

If there are seven or more dolls, at this point add aunt, cousin, etc. Be sure that you remem-ber where they go look-ing for Marysia.

Hold up doll set. Move around as though look-ing around yard. Take next doll (third smallest) apart, but keep remain-ing two dolls hidden in left hand.

Put Older Sister in a spot indicating village.

"Here I am," she said, "and here is Baby Sister—hiding under my skirts!"

And now, we must put the dolls together again. Who comes after Marysia? And where did she go?
(Go and get Older Sister from the village and continue until set is again complete.)

Hold up second smallest doll, with smallest doll inside. Open up the doll and show tiny, inmost doll.

At the end of the story, put the set together again by asking questions, and when the children respond correctly, point to one who has given the right answer and ask that child to go and get the doll. It becomes a memory game and gives at least a few of the children the opportunity to handle the dolls.

Trouble Dolls

Recently, tiny sets of wooden dolls, each roughly but individually carved and packed in small decorated boxes of lightweight wood, have appeared in gift stores and curio shops. Their country of origin is usually Guatemala, and tucked inside each box is a slip of paper stating that these are "trouble dolls," used by parents to get rid of their child's or children's troubles.

This is a simplified explanation for an old custom that has a very long and complex history. Suffice it to say that such sets of dolls were (and occasionally still are) used by many of the indigenous peoples of Central America to cure a child or group of children who had suffered a fright or a worrisome trouble and showed signs of unease, illness, or great unhappiness. It was believed that such children were in danger of losing their souls unless a healing process took place.

In most cases, a professional healer *(curandero* or *curandera)* was called upon, and he or she reenacted the events that caused the fright or trouble, using dolls for the characters in the story. Usually, each child being "cured" was told to put a doll representing himself or herself, or a doll representing the person, animal, or thing that had caused the fright, or both, into the box. After this, the healer said a prayer, put the cover on the box, and took it away, often to bury it at the spot where the fright or trouble occurred. This physical act surely did relieve many a child's worries.

The dolls had to be made of a special wood, often referred to as "sacred" among the various peoples. Sometimes they were entirely of wood and roughly painted; in other cases they had bits of cloth, hair, or other things attached.

I have used a set of "trouble dolls" in storytelling with small groups of children, particularly during family story hours held in the early evening. I invent a series of troubles, or ask the children to invent them, or to tell me of real frights they have had. They then come up, in turn, and put the dolls one by one into the box. When all of the dolls are in, I close the box and put it away.

The following story is typical of those I have spontaneously invented.

Nothing But Trouble

In a small town in Guatemala, on the side of a mountain, lived a small group of families, and in each of those families there were some children. Every day those children went about their tasks, going for water or for firewood, hoeing or weeding in the fields, or watching out for their younger brothers and sisters.

One afternoon, everything seemed to go wrong. Antonio was sent to get some firewood. He gathered a lot of fine sticks and dried branches and tied them in a bundle to carry on his head. But as he walked home through the dusky silence of the forest, a large man stepped out of the bushes and frightened Antonio so much, he dropped the bundle and ran home in terror. It was only one of the men from the village on the other side of the mountain, but Antonio had not stopped to look. He was sure it was a giant.

Maria was minding her baby brother, Pepito, and took him with her when she went to get water from the spring. She had filled her water jar and was balancing it on her head, when suddenly Pepito rushed off toward the edge of the precipice. Maria dropped her water jar and leaped after her brother, catching him just in time. Her heart pounded inside her all the way home, and she cried because she had broken the water jar.

Juanito and Rosa worked side by side in the cornfield, weeding and hoeing the new corn plants so they looked like neat green dolls standing in rows and waving their arms. The children did not see the bull slip out of their neighbor's pasture. Only when they heard a funny snort did they look up from their work. There was the bull, staring at them with his fierce eyes and pawing the ground only a few feet away.

Juanito and Rosa ran as fast as rabbits, leaping over the corn rows. When they reached home they were still howling and shrieking with fright.

"This day has brought nothing but trouble," said the parents that evening. "We must do something to cure our frightened children."

They called in the healing woman, the *curandera,* and she brought out her chips of sacred wood. Out of them she fashioned a set of tiny dolls. From the scraps and shavings she built a small fire and set the children around it, so they could smell the smoke.

"Tell me how you were frightened," said the healing woman.

And each of the children told her.

Then the *curandera* took the dolls, one by one, and acted out the stories the children had told her.

(At this point, if you wish, ask for volunteers from the child audience to act out or narrate the parts of the children. Simply say something like: Would you like to be Maria? Then tell me, or show me, what frightened Maria. Would you pretend you are Antonio? Then tell me, or show me, what happened to him.)

"Now it is time to cover up the troubles and frights and put them away for good," said the *curandera.*

She asked the children, one by one, to put the dolls into the box.

(Have the child volunteers do this.)

Then she closed the cover and put the box away, and the troubles were gone.

(Close box and put it away.)

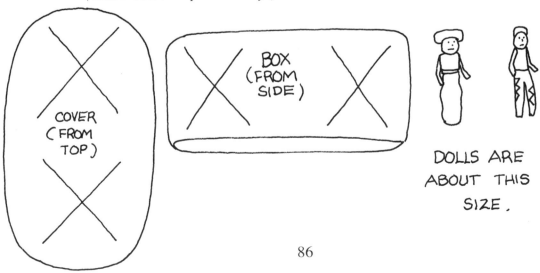

COVER
(FROM TOP)

BOX
(FROM SIDE)

DOLLS ARE
ABOUT THIS
SIZE.

Why the Years Are Named for Animals

There are many versions of the story that tells why the years are named for animals in almost all areas of south and southeast Asia. The Chinese have had, as part of their zodiac since early recorded time, the "twelve terrestrial branches," a method of dividing time into twelve segments. Some experts say that the method of computing years in cycles of twelve, using the animal names of these branches, began in the Han dynasty. Other experts state that the custom was probably brought to China by the Turks. One source insists that the first explicit mention of the custom of naming years for animals can be found in a history of the T'ang dynasty, where it is recorded that an envoy from the nation of Kirghiz spoke of events occurring in the Year of the Rabbit or the Year of the Horse.

Some versions of the tale refer simply to a godlike king or emperor who gives a party or reception and invites the animals to come. Other variants give the major role to Buddha. In some cases, the main emphasis is on arguments among the animals about who shall arrive first to the invited place. Dorothy O. Van Woerkom's picture book *The Rat, the Ox and the Zodiac* is a good example of the latter.

Still other versions emphasize the quarrel between Cat and Dog or between Cat and Rat, with Dog or Rat giving Cat incorrect information about Buddha's (or the emperor's) request; the result being that Cat arrives too late and therefore there is no Year of the Cat. *Twelve Years, Twelve Animals* by Yoshiko Samuel and *The Cat Who Went to Heaven* by Elizabeth Coatsworth both use this motif of the left-out cat.

The following story is one I developed from an oral telling I first heard in a Japanese temple, as translated by Sachiko Saionji (now Watanabe). I added a few details from other variants and from reading Buddhist scriptures.

A long time ago, the Buddha was sitting and meditating under his sacred *bo* tree. He knew that his time on earth was about to come to an end. Soon he would attain supreme and absolute wisdom and pass into Nirvana, the highest Heaven.

As he sat, he looked at the beauty of life all around him—especially the animals and other living creatures.

"Wouldn't it be fine," he thought, "if all of these living things could visit me for one last farewell and pay homage to the Enlightened One?"

So he sent an invitation to the four corners of the earth, asking all of the animals and creatures of the earth—one of each kind—to come to him on a certain day at a certain time, under the *bo* tree.

Then he sat and waited.

But when the day and the hour arrived, only twelve animals had shown up. For a moment, an angry thought welled up in the Buddha.

"What if a flood were to come and destroy the earth and all the creatures on it?" he wondered. The Buddha remembered the flood brought down by the evil god Mara.

But the thought was hardly formed when the Buddha recalled his mission on earth.

"I am here to teach respect for life," he said. "I do not wish to destroy even the tiniest of creatures.

"Rather than calling for the punishment of the careless and indifferent animals who did not come, I must think of some way to honor these twelve faithful animals who *did* come," decided the Buddha.

He thought and thought and then announced his plan: Henceforth, the years would be named for the twelve faithful animals who had answered his call. The years would be named in the order that the animals had arrived.

And so, to this very day, in the countries of Asia where the teachings of Buddha spread, the people call the years by the names of those twelve animals, according to the order in which they came, to honor the Buddha:

First, the Year of the Rat
Second, the Year of the Ox
Third, the Year of the Tiger

Hold up the
animal figurines
one by one.

Fourth, the Year of the Rabbit
Fifth, the Year of the Dragon
Sixth, the Year of the Snake
Seventh, the Year of the Horse
Eighth, the Year of the Sheep
Ninth, the Year of the Monkey
Tenth, the Year of the Rooster
Eleventh, the Year of the Dog
Twelfth, the Year of the Pig or Boar

And when the cycle is completed, it begins over again.

RAT	TIGER	DRAGON	HORSE	MONKEY	DOG
1900	1902	1904	1906	1908	1910
1912	1914	1916	1918	1920	1922
1924	1926	1928	1930	1932	1934
1936	1938	1940	1942	1944	1946
1948	1950	1952	1954	1956	1958
1960	1962	1964	1966	1968	1970
1972	1974	1976	1978	1980	1982
1984	1986	1988	1990	1992	1994

OX	RABBIT	SNAKE	SHEEP	ROOSTER	PIG or BOAR
1901	1903	1905	1907	1909	1911
1913	1915	1917	1919	1921	1923
1925	1927	1929	1931	1933	1935
1937	1939	1941	1943	1945	1947
1949	1951	1953	1955	1957	1959
1961	1963	1965	1967	1969	1971
1973	1975	1977	1979	1981	1983
1985	1987	1989	1991	1993	1995

Stories with Dolls or Figurines—Bibliography

Dolls

Benet, Sula. *Song, Dance and Customs of Peasant Poland.* New York: Roy Publishers, 1951.

Boehn, Max von. *Dolls and Puppets.* London: G. G. Harrap, 1932.

Dintzes, Lev A. *Russkaĭa Glinĭanaĭa Igrushka.* Moscow, 1936.

Hartmann, Günther. *Litjoko: Puppen der Karaja, Brasilien.* Berlin: Musem für Völkerkunde, 1973.

Holmer, Nils M., and S. Henry Wassén. *The Complete Mu-Igala in Picture Writing: A Native Record of a Cuna Indian Medicine Song.* Etnologiske Studier 21. Göteborg, 1953.

Gillen, John. "Magical-Fright." *Guatemala,* Vol. 2–3, No. 3 (August 1940).

Igrushka: Eĭa Istoria I Znachenie. Moscow, 1912.

Kolberg, Oskar. *Dzieła Wszystkie.* 66 vols. Wrocław: Polskie Towarzystwo Ludoznawcze, 1961–79.

Mendoza, Virginia de. "El Mal de Espanto y Manera de Curarlo en Algunos Lugares en México." *Boletín de la Sociedad de Folklore de Tucuman,* No. 5 (1951).

Rodriguez Rouanet, Franciso. "Ojeo, Susto, Hijillo y Acuas; Enfermedades del Indígena Kekchi." *Tradiciones de Guatemala,* Vol. 1 (1968), pp. 43–46.

Russian Toys. Moscow: Progress Publishers, 1974.

A story that works well, using one of the Russian nesting dolls, is "Vasilissa the Beautiful," which is available in a number of editions. (Locate through indexes cited under Sources of Stories, p. 115.)

The film *Matrioska* (16 mm, color, 5 minutes), animated by Jana Bendova and Co Hoedeman (National Film Board of Canada, 1970), is very effective in a program with the stories in this section.

Animal Zodiac

Chavannes, Edouard. *Contes et Légendes du Bouddhisme Chinois.* Paris: Bossard, 1921.

Coatsworth, Elizabeth. *The Cat Who Went to Heaven.* Illustrated by Lynd Ward. New York: Macmillan Co., 1930.

Eberhard, Wolfram. *Folktales of China.* Chicago: University of Chicago Press, 1965.

Samuel, Yoshiko. *Twelve Years, Twelve Animals.* Illustrated by Margo Locke. Nashville, Tenn.: Abingdon, 1972.

Shah, Idries. ''Born Under the Sign of the Donkey.'' In his *Exploits of the Incomparable Mulla Nasrudin.* New York: Simon and Schuster, 1967.

Ting, Nai Tung, and Hsü Lee-hsia Ting. *Chinese Folk Narratives.* San Francisco: Chinese Materials and Research Aids Service Center, 1975.

Van Woerkom, Dorothy O. *The Rat, The Ox and the Zodiac.* Illustrated by Errol Le Cain. New York: Crown, 1976.

Wang, Ch'ung. ''Wu-shih.'' (The Nature of Things.) In his *Lun-Heng,* translated by Alfred Forke, Book III, Chapter 5. 1907. Reprint. New York: Paragon, 1962.

Williams, Charles A. S. *Outlines of Chinese Symbolism.* Peiping: Customs College Press, 1931. Reprint. New York: Julian Press, 1960.

PART FOUR

Finger-Play Stories

In many cultures, these are the first stories babies get to hear. The narrative of "This Little Pig Went to Market" might seem tame and boring to a five- or six-year-old, but to a baby just discovering language at the same time as fingers and toes, it is high drama.

Every adult should have a few of these stories ready to use at a moment's notice. They are perfect for calming or entertaining children in times of stress or when traveling. I could cite at least a dozen instances when two bits of paper, torn from a tissue in my purse, have been transformed magically into two little birds and have provided distraction and fun when harassed parents and fellow travelers most needed it.

Many of these finger-play stories are best suited to family storytelling in the home, but there are some that can be used effectively with small groups of children in public situations as well. I have included here a few personal favorites. The bibliography lists collections that can be used for additional suggestions.

Two Little _____* Birds

I like to use this story with four- and five-year-olds. That seems to be the perfect age for it. Once the children have caught on to the trick, they love to try it out themselves on anyone who will watch and listen.

Two little _____* birds	*Before beginning story, paste a piece of tissue or paper over the nail of each index finger. Hold the two index fingers out and keep the other fingers and thumbs clenched in fists.*
Sitting on a hill;	*Rest index fingers, stretched out, on a table, lap, or other surface.*
This one named Jack;	*Lift up right index finger.*
This one named Jill.	*Lift up left index finger.*
Fly away, Jack!	*Lift right hand over right shoulder and while it is there, curl index finger under and instead stretch out middle finger. Bring right hand, with middle finger extended, down to rest on table.*
Fly away, Jill!	*Do the same with left hand, again substituting middle finger for index finger as the one held out.*
Come back, Jack!	*Lift right hand over shoulder and while doing so, pull back middle finger and extend index finger, so the paper shows again. Place extended index finger on table.*
Come back, Jill!	*Do the same with the left hand.*

*Make the birds the color of the tissue or other paper that you have handy and name them accordingly, e.g., blue, yellow, white, red, black.

The Pigs

This is slightly adapted from the collection of Emilie Poulsson, first published in 1893, but still a good source for finger plays.

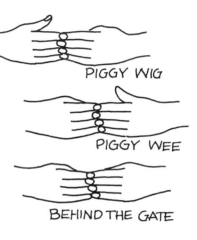

Piggie Wig and Piggie Wee,
Hungry pigs as pigs could be,
For their dinner had to wait
Down behind the garden gate.

Place hands on table or lap, tips of fingers slightly overlapping and thumbs behind. Lift up right thumb for Piggie Wig and left thumb for Piggie Wee. Hold them up until you say "Down behind" and then drop them down behind hands.

Piggie Wig and Piggie Wee
Climbed the barnyard gate to see.
They peeped through the gate so high,
But no dinner could they spy.

Open space between index and middle fingers and let thumbs peep through.

Piggie Wig and Piggie Wee
Got down, sad as pigs could be;
But the gate soon opened wide
And they scampered forth outside.

Drop thumbs and close space between index and middle fingers.

Open hands.

Make fists, with thumbs thrusting out, and slide hands forward in twisting motion.

94

Piggie Wig and Piggie Wee,
Were delighted then to see
Dinner ready not far off—
Such a full and tempting trough!

Lift up right and left thumbs and wiggle them. Lift hands and cup them to make trough.

TROUGH

Piggie Wig and Piggie Wee,
Greedy pigs as pigs could be,
For their dinner ran pell-mell;
In the trough both piggies fell!

Lift up right and left thumbs and wiggle them.

IN THEY
FELL

Drop thumbs very suddenly behind hands.

The Owl and the Mice

I have adapted this from Maud Burnham's *Rhymes for Little Hands*, another old collection that has served as an inspiration to many tellers who use finger-play stories.

An owl sat alone
   on the branch of a tree;
And he was as quiet
   as quiet could be;

Hold left arm out; make fist with right hand and rest fist on middle part of left arm. Use a soft, whispery voice to say the words.

It was night and his eyes
   were open like this!
He looked all around;
   not a thing did he miss.

Bring hands to eyes and circle them, as though looking through binoculars. While looking, move head from side to side. Make voice even softer and more mysterious.

Two mice started creeping
   up the trunk of that tree;
They stopped below the branch
   to see what they could see.

Hold left arm straight down. With right index and middle fingers, "creep" from bottom of arm (on inner side) up as far as elbow joint. Keep voice to a whisper.

Said the solemn old owl,
   "Whoo!   Whoo!   Whoo!
Whoo!"
Up jumped the two mice
   and down the tree they flew!

Bring hands up to circle eyes again. Use loud voice for owl's call. Drop left arm so it is hanging straight down. Move right index and middle fingers from inner part of elbow down to wrist, in one bound.

The Crab

This is a Kashubian-Polish finger game. It is meant to be used with very young children from one to three years old.

Here comes a little pinching crab;
Wherever he goes he makes a grab.
He goes far, then he comes near;
He goes there, then he moves over here—
  to the hands,
  to the mouth like a rose;
  to the pink bellybutton
  and down to the toes,
  and then up that crab goes
  to pinch off _____* nose!

Spread out fingers of hand, crablike, with thumb and index finger opening and closing like pincers. Gently pinch hair on baby's head, then one set of baby's fingers.

Pinch an ear, then a knee.
Pinch other set of fingers.
Pinch baby's lips.
Pinch baby's navel.
Pinch one set of toes.

Pinch baby's nose.

The pinching should be more like gentle tweaking than actual pinching.

*Use the name of the baby here.

Finger-Play Stories—Bibliography

Brown, Marc. *Finger Rhymes*. New York: Dutton, 1980.

Burnham, Maud. *Rhymes for Little Hands*. Springfield, Mass.: Milton Bradley, 1906.

Carlson, Bernice Wells. *Listen! And Help Tell the Story*. Nashville, Tenn.: Abingdon, 1965.

Glazer, Tom. *Eye Winker, Tom Tinker, Chin Chopper*. New York: Doubleday & Co., 1973.

Grayson, Marion. *Let's Do Fingerplays*. Washington: Robert B. Luce, 1962.

Matterson, Elizabeth. *Games for the Very Young: Finger Plays and Nursery Rhymes*. New York: American Heritage (McGraw Hill), 1969.

Poulsson, Emilie. *Finger Plays*. New York: Lothrop, 1893. Reprint. New York: Dover Publications, 1971.

Yamaguchi, Marianne. *Finger Plays*. New York: Holt, Rinehart, 1970.

PART FIVE

Riddling

Riddling is practiced by most cultural groups, either for pure entertainment or to teach the subtleties of language, especially symbolic language, in a pleasurable way. Since many African storytelling sessions in family compounds are preceded by riddling, it seems appropriate to insert a few African riddles here, ahead of the section on African thumb piano stories.

The session usually starts with the riddler saying something like: "I'll throw you a riddle!" or "Here's a riddle!" or "Catch the riddle!" The listener responds with: "I'll throw it [the answer] back!" or "I've got it!" or "I caught it!" The riddle is then posed, and answers are offered until the correct one is found or the person gives up. The riddling continues until no more riddles can be brought forward.

It is often at that point that the riddling session turns into a storytelling event, sometimes because a riddle or its answer has reminded a teller of a tale.

I frequently pose riddles before telling stories, especially when I am about to tell African tales. The following are some of my favorites, learned orally during the course of one of my trips to Africa, or from authentic print sources.

A Selection of African Riddles

1. Two birds can fly over two hundred trees. What are they?
   Eyes
2. I am small but I am not afraid to eat off the king's plate.
   Fly
3. I pass the living, they are silent;
   I pass the dead, they speak to me.
   Leaves
4. The red one is licking the black one's bottom.
   Fire and Cooking Pot
5. I am asked to bring it, and I bring it.
   I am asked to return it and I cannot, for I don't know where it came from.
   A hair from my head
6. The sad one has stopped crying;
   The compassionate friends are still weeping.
   Cloud and trees dripping after rain has stopped
7. I stay on the farm—I wear my clothes.
   I go to market—I go naked!
   Corn
8. I am a snake without head or tail.
   Road
9. I have no wings or legs but I can jump over a high wall.
   Voice
10. Give me work to do and I'll do it well;
    Ask me to rest and I'll start weeping!
    Sponge

Riddling—Bibliography

Aardema, Verna. *Ji-Nongo-Nongo Means Riddles.* Illustrated by Jerry Pinkney. New York: Four Winds, 1978.

Aarne, Antti. *Vergleichende Rätselforschungen.* Helsinki: Folklore Fellows, FF Communications, No. 26–28 (1918–1919).

Anya-Noa, Lucien. *Énigmes Betis.* Yaoundé, 196-.

Beier, Ulli. *The Moon Cannot Fight; Yoruba Children's Poems.* Ibadan: Mbari Publications, n.d.

Gowlett, D. F. ''Some Lozi Riddles and Tongue-Twisters Annotated and Analyzed.'' *African Studies,* Vol. 25 (1966), pp. 139–158.

Lebeuf, Jean Paul. *Devinettes Peules.* Cahiers de l'Homme, nouv. ser. 12. Paris: Mouton, 1972.

McDowell, John Holmes. *Children's Riddling.* Bloomington: Indiana University Press, 1979.

Riddles and Riddling. Issue edited by Elli Köngäs Maranda. *Journal of American Folklore,* Vol. 89 (April–June 1976).

PART SIX

Stories Using
Musical Instruments

The variety of musical instruments used in storytelling is large, ranging from the many forms of ancient lyres, harps, and lutes to more modern instruments made of brass bowls, metal pipes, or hollowed-out gourds. I refer now to folk tales or epics told by traditional storytellers using instruments to accompany their stories, not to the musical compositions of well-known composers (such as *Peter and the Wolf* by Prokofiev), in which certain instruments or musical themes represent characters or events in a story.

One of the most beautiful legends of how a group of tellers came to use a particular instrument is the story of the horse-head fiddle of Mongolia, recounted in a lovely picture book from Japan, available in English as *Suho and the White Horse*. Anyone with access to such a fiddle, and with the ability to play it, could provide a memorable and haunting storytelling session using that book.

Usually, one must have extensive musical training in order to do a good job of telling stories while using an instrument. However, some exceptions are the thumb piano, the drum, and simple wind instruments. These instruments can be played in very complex and beautiful patterns and melodies, but they are also easy to play in a simple way by the beginner.

I have had no formal musical training but have found it relatively easy to do thumb piano or drum stories from African folklore.

Africa Thumb Piano Stories

The thumb piano is an instrument unique to Africa. It is an idiophone, that is, an instrument with a sounding box that can be made of wood, reeds, gourds, turtle shells, sardine tins, or just about any hollow or concave object found in sub-Saharan Africa. The tongues (also called spikes or lamellae) are usually of metal but occasionally of reeds.

One of the common names for the thumb piano is *kalimba*. In parts of West Africa it is called a *sanza*. In Zambia, the larger type is called *kankobela* and the smaller, *ndandi*. Among the Bini people of Nigeria it is known as an *asologun*. Dan Ben-Amos, in his book *Sweet Words,* gives an explanation of the manner in which it is played and some of its history. A popular use of the thumb piano is to accompany story-telling.

In central and southern Africa the thumb piano is usually called an *mbira*. The Library of African Music in Grahamstown, South Africa, has a very large collection of *mbiras,* as well as thumb pianos from many other parts of Africa. Some of them can be seen in the film *Mapandangare, the Great Baboon*, featuring Andrew Tracey, son of Hugh Tracey, the founder of the library.

I first heard and saw the thumb piano used as a part of storytelling in Zambia, in a school about an hour's drive from Lusaka, where the children performed and told stories for me. One of the stories I heard was a version of the first story that follows, but I got only a very sketchy outline of it when I asked for a translation. Later, I found a tale with similar elements as the title story in Hugh Tracey's *The Lion on the Path and Other Stories*.

I have combined and adapted these two versions to create my own way of telling the tale to audiences who are not familiar with the response chants typically expected of African audiences. For those who wish to use the exact words and music as recorded from folk tellers, I recommend the Tracey version.

Strictly speaking, Rabbit should be called Hare, but I have stayed with the more familiar name in order to show the original connection to the Br'er Rabbit stories (in Spanish, *Tio Conejo*) brought by black Africans to the Americas.

If you feel you are not musical, do not be intimidated or fearful about telling thumb piano stories. The thumb piano is a folk instrument and can be played very easily by anyone with the ability to move his or her thumbs. The most common chants or accompaniments consist of three tone melodies repeated over and over. There are, of course, experts who can play the thumb piano beautifully, using very intricate musical patterns. They can be heard on the recording listed in the bibliography. However, in an African village, one is much more likely to encounter an ordinary person walking along and plunking softly on a thumb piano in a simple, repetitious, three-note song, spontaneously made up because the combination seemed pleasing to the ear.

Authentic, handmade thumb pianos can be purchased in museum shops, in African gift shops, or at the United Nations gift shop in New York, as well as at UNA-UNICEF shops throughout the country. A commercially produced version of the thumb piano is sold through the Children's Book and Music Center, 2500 Santa Monica Boulevard, Santa Monica, California 90404.

The Lion on the Path

There was once a farmer and his wife who lived together very happily, except that the wife was always getting lonesome. They had no children yet and she came from a big family and was used to having a lot of relatives around her. So she was always asking for permission to go off and visit her family.

One day the farmer and his wife were working in the field side by side, hoeing. It was very hot. The sun beat down on them until the wife thought she could stand it no longer.

"Husband, I want to go off and visit my family," she said.

"What? Again? You just went last week," he answered.

"I know, but I'm so tired and lonely."

"Very well, wife," said the husband. "I'll finish the work for both of us. But, wife, I want you to remember to take the path that runs above the village—the longer one that we don't usually take. Don't go by the shorter path below the village, where we usually walk, because of late, people have told me there is a lion on that path."

"Oh, husband, I know the way," said the wife, and she put down her hoe and took off. But the truth of the matter is, she had not been listening.

The husband continued to hoe for a time and then he felt a funny feeling inside his middle.

"I think my wife has taken the wrong path," he said.

He put down his hoe and ran to the edge of the village.

Sure enough, where the two paths divided, he saw the footprints of his wife in the path running below the village—the one with a lion on it!

He tore down the path and when he came to a curve where there was a huge rock, he stepped around it, and what should he see but his wife and, facing her, a huge lion about to pounce on her!

The farmer was very quick thinking, so he snatched up his *mbira* from the place where it always hung, tied to his belt. He began to play a tune.

(*Begin playing the* mbira.)

The lion stopped looking at the farmer's wife and began to listen to the music, as though he were hypnotized.

"Run, wife! Get out of here and don't look back!" ordered the farmer.

She turned and ran and didn't look back to see how her husband would get away.

The farmer continued to play and then he said: "Now I must think of a way to get out."

He thought for a moment and then remembered the big rock in the curve of the path.

"I'll take a step or two behind that rock and then run for it," he decided.

He stepped backward toward the rock.

But the lion wanted to hear that *mbira* music and he crept forward, so that he was as close to the farmer as he had been before.

105

"That wasn't far enough backward," thought the farmer. "I'll take three giant steps and then I'll surely be hidden." He took three enormous strides backward, but just as he was about to turn and run, there was that lion, creeping up, until he was as close to the farmer as he'd been before.

"I'll never get out of here," moaned the farmer.

He continued to play the *mbira* for a long time, until he thought his thumbs would fall off. The lion continued to stare at him, hypnotized by the music.

(Play mbira *very slowly.)*

Just when the farmer was about to give up hope, he heard a voice say: "Psst!"

The farmer looked down, out of the corner of his eye, and there at his side was Rabbit.

"I've always wanted an *mbira,"* said Rabbit. "If you give me yours, I'll help you get out of here and away from the lion."

"Gladly!" said the farmer. He reached down very carefully, without stopping his playing, and handed the *mbira* to Rabbit, who picked it up in his paws and kept on playing as nice as you please.

Lion was now staring at Rabbit and listening intently to the music.

The farmer turned and ran, and he didn't look back to see how Rabbit would get out of there.

Rabbit played nicely for a while, and then he began to take hops backward. Lion continued creeping along forward, so he was always close to Rabbit.

(Play mbira *more slowly, in two notes.)*

But Rabbit seemed to pay no mind and just went on hopping backward . . . and backward . . . and backward . . . until—*pop!* Rabbit landed right in his hole in the ground.

(Stop playing mbira.)

Lion shook his mane and said: "I thought I saw a woman, and then a man, and then a Rabbit standing in front of me. And now I see only an *mbira.* I can't eat that."

Then Lion shook his mane again and said: "Oh, well. I guess I have to go to another path to look for my dinner."

And he did.

Rabbit and Hyena Play the *Sanza*

This is an adaptation of a story recorded by René Guillot in the Belgian Congo, now Zaire. In the original transcription, the instrument mentioned is a *balafon,* a kind of xylophone. However, the thumb piano is also mentioned in the stories from the same general area, so it seemed appropriate to substitute it. The teller could use either a *balafon* or a *sanza,* whichever is most readily available.

It was a time of great famine. All the animals in the bush were having a difficult time finding enough to eat. All except Rabbit, that is. Somehow or other, he always managed to find good food and plenty of it.

One day, when Rabbit's food supply dwindled down to nothing, he fashioned a cage out of reeds and vines. Then he took his *sanza,* a pail of water, a small broom made of twigs, and his cage, and carried them off to the edge of the bush. There, he began to play a tune and sing:

> Come one, come all.   *Play thumb piano*
> Come and dance to the music   *with both hands.*
>   of my fine *sanza.*

Well, before long a small flock of Guinea Hens came out from the bush. They began to dance, twisting and turning, bobbing up and down, and twitching their tails. They danced until Rabbit paused in his playing of the *sanza.*

When they had caught their breaths, the Guinea Hens turned to Rabbit.

''Why are you playing the *sanza?*'' asked one of them.

''It has been such a hard time of late, I thought you needed cheering up,'' answered Rabbit.

''Isn't he kind!'' clucked some of the Guinea Hens.

''But why do you have that pail of water?'' asked one of them.

''I know you get thirsty after a good dance,'' said Rabbit. ''I thought I'd have the water handy for you here, so you wouldn't have to go way down to the water hole.''

"What a thoughtful creature," clucked the remaining Guinea Hens, until suddenly, they spotted the broom.

"What is that doing here?"

"You know how you stir up a lot of dust when you dance," said Rabbit. "I wanted you to enjoy your dancing without having your lovely feathers covered with dust."

"That is one of the friendliest gestures we have ever seen," cackled the Guinea Hens.

Just then, a few of them noticed the cage.

"Why do you need a cage?" they wanted to know.

"It's a shelter," said Rabbit. "The rainy season is about to start and if it begins to rain while you are dancing, I want to be sure you have a place to run quickly to protect yourself from the downpour."

"We have never known anyone as generous as you are," murmured the Guinea Hens as they fluffed their feathers in preparation for the next dance.

Rabbit began playing once more on the *sanza* and singing in his cajoling voice:

Come and dance,   *Play* sanza *using*
While you have a chance.   *both hands.*
It is not every day
That I am here to play
    on the *sanza.*

When the Guinea Hens were completely taken up with the steps of their dance, Rabbit stopped playing with one paw, but continued to play with the other. With his free paw, he picked up the broom, dipped it into the water, and sprinkled it over the Guinea Hens.

"It's starting to rain, my beauties," he cried. "Come into the shelter."

Foolish Guinea Hens! Several of them dashed for the cage and as soon as they were inside, Rabbit stopped playing the *sanza* and slid the door of the cage shut. The rest of the flock went shrieking and fluttering off into the bush.

"Ha! Now I have enough food to last me for several days," gloated Rabbit. He pulled the cage of cackling Guinea Hens along toward his home at the edge of the bush. He had almost arrived there, ready to hide the cage from prying eyes, when who should come along but Hyena.

"Well, well," said Hyena. "How is it that even in times of famine, some people get more than their share of food?"

"Oh, it was just a trick I tried out," said Rabbit modestly. "The results were not too bad, eh?"

Hyena pleaded with Rabbit to tell him how he had done it and Rabbit, in his good-natured way, told Hyena all about it.

"I'd like to try that," said Hyena.

Rabbit laughed. He knew Hyena was a pretty stupid fellow, and was sure not to get it right. Still, he offered to loan Hyena the *sanza,* the pail of water, and the broom.

"But you'll have to make your own cage," he said to Hyena.

Hyena set to work and constructed a large, strong cage of reeds and vines—twice as big as the one Rabbit had used. He pulled the cage to a clearing at the edge of the bush and then set the pail of water and the broom beside it. Finally, he took the *sanza* in his hands and began to play and sing in his high, shrieking voice:

Come one, come all.   *Play thumb piano*
Come and dance to the music *with both hands.*
    of my fine *sanza.*

Before long, the flock of Guinea Hens came out of the bush and began to dance. They strutted and bobbed and twisted their tails.

Hyena paused in his singing and then the Guinea Hens saw who it was that was playing and singing. They eyed Hyena suspiciously.

"Why are you playing the *sanza?*" they asked.

"Have you forgotten it's a time of famine?" asked Hyena. "I have to figure out some way of getting my food, just like everyone else."

"Oh, is that so?" clucked the Guinea Hens. Then they spied the pail of water, the broom, and the cage.

"Why do you have those things here?" they asked.

"You stupid Guinea Hens," said Hyena. "Don't you realize that's for me to use later on? I shall sprinkle water and it will be like rain falling. Then you must run and take shelter in the cage. Don't you understand?"

"Oh, yes!" said the Guinea Hens. "We understand very well."

"Fine! Then let's begin the dancing again," suggested Hyena.

He began to play the *sanza* once more and sang in shrieks and yowls:

Come and dance,   *Play* sanza *with*
While you have a chance.   *both hands.*
It is not every day
That I am here to play
  the *sanza*.

But the Guinea Hens did not begin to dance. They simply stood there, moving from one foot to the other.

Hyena stopped his playing and singing.

"You silly creatures," he shouted. "Don't you remember? You're supposed to dance, and then when the water falls, you're supposed to go into the cage for shelter."

"But we don't know how to do it," tittered one of the Guinea Hens. "You see, we've never walked into such a shelter before."

"Of all the stupid ones, you are the most stupid," shrieked Hyena. "You just duck your head down, like this, and start to walk in." Hyena lowered his head and thrust it into the cage.

"Oh, we know how to duck our heads and get that part in," said one of the Guinea Hens. "But the rest of us—how will we all fit in?"

Grumbling and snarling, Hyena crawled into the cage.

"Like this!" he said.

Snap! The Guinea Hens shut the door tight and Hyena was captured in his own cage.

One of the Guinea Hens picked up the *sanza* and began to play, while the rest of the flock danced on.

*And do you know, I think they are still at it. I went by last year and there was Hyena, still in his cage, with the Guinea Hens dancing around it.

*This is a traditional ending to stories in parts of central Africa.

Stories Using Musical Instruments— Bibliography

Barker, W. H., and C. Sinclair. *West African Folk Tales*. London: G. G. Harrap, 1917. "The Hunter and the Tortoise" in this collection is a thumb piano story. Courlander (see below) cites it as the source for his story, "The Singing Tortoise," but it is actually quite different in mood.

Ben-Amos, Dan. *Sweet Words: Storytelling in Benin*. Philadelphia: Institute for the Study of Human Issues, 1975.

Courlander, Harold, and George Herzog. *The Cow-Tail Switch and Other West African Stories*. New York: Holt, Rinehart, 1947. Compare "The Singing Tortoise" with the Barker and Sinclair, Jagendorf and Boggs, and Thoby-Marcelin versions.

Courlander, Harold. *The Piece of Fire and Other Haitian Tales*. New York: Harcourt, Brace, 1964. "Merisier, Stronger than the Elephants" is a story of the origin of the drum.

Guillot, René. *La Brousse et la Bête*. Paris: Delagrave, 1950.

————. *Au Pays des Bêtes Sauvages*. Paris: Rageot (Éditions de l'Amitié), 1948.

Jagendorf, M. A., and R. S. Boggs. *The King of the Mountains*. New York: Vanguard, 1971. "Clever Little Turtle" is a Brazilian story with motifs similar to "The Hunter and the Tortoise," "The Singing Tortoise," and "The Singing Turtle."

Otsuka, Yuzo. *Suho and the White Horse*. Translated by Ann Herring. Illustrated by Suekichi Akaba. New York: Viking Penguin, 1981. The story of the origin of the horse-head fiddle, an instrument used by Mongolian storytellers.

Robinson, Adjai. *Singing Tales of Africa*. Illustrated by Christine Price. New York: Charles Scribner's Sons, 1974. Each story has at least one song as part of the action. "Ojumiri and the Giant" works best when one has a *balanji*, a type of xylophone, to play in the appropriate parts.

Serwadda, Moses, and Hewitt Pantaleoni. *Songs and Stories from Uganda*. Illustrated by Leo and Diane Dillon. New York: T. Y. Crowell, 1974. All of the tales have musical segments. "Ttimba" should be accompanied by drumming; "Nsangi" works well with a thumb piano.

Thoby-Marcelin, Philippe. *The Singing Turtle and Other Tales from Haiti*. New York: Farrar, Straus & Giroux, 1971. It is interesting to compare the title story in its African, West Indian, and Brazilian versions.

Tooze, Ruth. *Three Tales of Monkey*. Illustrated by R. P. Schmidt. New York: John Day, 1967. Four monkeys invent the flute, the lute, the cymbal, and the drum.

Tracey, Hugh. *The Lion on the Path and Other Stories*. London: Routledge and Kegan Paul, 1967. Many of the tales in this collection are meant to be accompanied by the thumb piano, drum, or just singing.

Wolkstein, Diane. *The Magic Orange Tree and Other Haitian Folktales*. New York: Alfred A. Knopf, 1978. Eight of the stories have songs, for which the music and words are given.

Film and Recordings

Musical Instruments, 2: Reeds, Mbira, recorded by Hugh Tracey. Music of Africa series. Washington: Traditional Music Documentation Project, 1972. This can be ordered by writing to the Project's offices at 3740 Kanawha St., NW, Washington, D.C. 20015.

Mapandangare, the Brave Baboon. 16 mm color film. Produced by Producers' Film Marketing. Distributed in U.S. by Film Fair Communications, Los Angeles.

Some Suggestions for Storytellers

I personally believe storytelling can best be learned by listening to good tellers and then practicing what one has learned through observation. However, there are handbooks and other books that can be helpful, especially for the beginning storyteller, or the one who would like to try telling in a different setting or with a new method. The following books can be of assistance in many cases.

Storytelling Handbooks

Baker, Augusta, and Ellin Greene. *Storytelling: Art and Technique*. New York: R. R. Bowker Co., 1977. Best suited for librarians planning story hour programs. Part 3—Selection and Part 4—Preparation are also useful for parents and other storytellers. Appendix 2 has good lists of stories to tell, arranged by age group and type.

Bauer, Caroline Feller. *Handbook for Storytellers*. Chicago: American Library Association, 1977.

There are quite a number of other fine handbooks, each with its own special lists and guidelines. Most of them are mentioned in the bibliographies of the above two books and can be tracked down in that way.

Reading-Aloud Handbooks

Kimmel, Margaret, and Elizabeth Segal. *For Reading Out Loud: A Guide to Sharing Books with Children*. New York: Delacorte, 1983. This would be the first choice for teachers and librarians.

Trelease, Jim. *The Read-Aloud Handbook*. New York: Viking Penguin, 1982. A very good guide for parents.

Storytelling Inspiration

Sawyer, Ruth. *The Way of the Storyteller*. New York: Viking Penguin, 1977.
Shedlock, Marie. *The Art of the Storyteller*. New York: Dover Publications, 1951.

These are paperback reprints of books that have been around a long time. They are still the best for conveying the special power and the joys of storytelling.

Storytelling Organizations

The National Association for the Preservation and Perpetuation of Storytelling, Box 112, Jonesborough, Tenn. 37659

Storytelling Periodicals

National Storytelling Journal, published by NAPPS, Box 112, Jonesborough, Tenn. 37659.
Parabola, published by the Society for the Study of Myth and Tradition, 150 Fifth Ave., New York, N.Y. 10011
The Yarnspinner, published by NAPPS, Box 112, Jonesborough, Tenn. 37659

Historical Background

Pellowski, Anne. *The World of Storytelling*. New York: R. R. Bowker Co., 1977.

For those who wish to know how storytelling began in most parts of the world, and how it continues in its varied forms to the present day. Section 14 gives suggestions for more authentic storytelling.

Sources of Stories

Indexes

Macdonald, Margaret Read. *The Storyteller's Sourcebook: A Subject, Title and Motif Index to Folklore Collections for Children*. Detroit: Gale (Neal-Schuman), 1982. Useful for the teller who is searching for a specific motif, subject, or story from a particular national or ethnic group.

Stories: A List of Stories to Tell and to Read Aloud. 7th ed. Edited by Marilyn Iarusso. New York: New York Public Library, 1977.

Stories to Tell: A List of Stories With Annotations. 5th ed. Edited by Jeanne Hardendorff. Baltimore: Enoch Pratt Free Library, 1965.

Stories to Tell Children: A Selected List. 8th ed. Edited by Laura Cathon. Pittsburgh: University of Pittsburgh Press, 1974.

See also the appendices in Baker and Greene, and in Bauer (above).

Collections

The following collections are personal favorites. About half of my repertoire comes from these books. The titles listed under each entry are stories I tell from that collection. The remainder of my stories are, for the most part, from oral sources.

Every teller should begin his or her own search for stories, first by listening to other storytellers, and then by searching out old and new collections such as the ones below, both in print and out of print.

Asbjornsen, Peter C., and Jorgen Moe. *East of the Sun and West of the Moon*. New York: Macmillan Co., 1963. Other good editions are available.
"The Giant Who Had No Heart in His Body"; "The Squire's Bride."

Bialik, Hayyim Nahman. *And It Came To Pass*. Translated by Herbert Danby. Illustrated by Howard Simon. New York: Hebrew Publishing Co., 1938.
"The Bee."

Carrick, Valery. *Picture Folk Tales*. Reprint. New York: Dover Publications, 1967.

"The Bun"; "The Crab and the Jaguar."

Colwell, Eileen. *A Storyteller's Choice*. New York: Henry Z. Walck, 1964.
"Lazy Tok."

Courlander, Harold. *The Tiger's Whisker and Other Tales and Legends from Asia and the Pacific*. New York: Harcourt Brace, 1959.
"The Tiger's Whisker"; "The Musician of Tagaung."

Duvoisin, Roger. *The Three Sneezes and Other Swiss Tales*. New York: Alfred A. Knopf, 1957.
"Pig Music."

Farjeon, Eleanor. *The Little Bookroom*. Oxford and New York: Oxford University Press, 1955.
"The Seventh Princess"; "Young Kate."

Fillmore, Parker. *The Shepherd's Nosegay: Stories from Finland and Czechoslovakia*. New York: Harcourt Brace, 1958.
"Clever Manka"; "Mary, Mary, So Contrary"; "The Shepherd's Nosegay."

Grimm, Jakob, and Wilhelm Grimm. *Household Stories*. Translated by Lucy Crane. Reprint. New York: Dover Publications, 1963.
"The Goose Girl."

Hatch, Mary. *Thirteen Danish Tales*. New York: Harcourt Brace, 1947.
"Fiddivaw."

Jacobs, Joseph. *English Fold and Fairy Tales*. New York: Putnam, 1904.
"Cap o' Rushes"; "Teeny-Tiny"; "Mr. Miacca"; "Master of All Masters."

Kelsey, Alice Geer. *Once the Hodja*. New York: Longmans, 1943.
"A Guest for Halil"; "Three Fridays."

Ritchie, Alice. *The Treasure of Li Po*. New York: Harcourt Brace, 1949.
"Two of Everything."

Sandburg, Carl. *Rootabaga Stories*. New York: Harcourt Brace, 1974 (Reprint).
"The Story of Blixie Bimber and the Power of the Gold Buckskin Whincher"; "How the Letter X Got into the Alphabet."

Serwadda, Moses, and Hewitt Pantaleoni. *Songs and Stories from Uganda*. New York: T. Y. Crowell, 1974.
"Tweriire"; "Ttimba."

Tracey, Hugh. *The Lion on the Path and Other Stories*. New York: Praeger, 1968.
"The Cat Who Came Indoors"; "The Girl and the Crocodile."